# Paid *in* Chocolate

*Tales from a Counselor's Chair*

JOHNNA ANNE GURR MS, LPC

authorHOUSE

AuthorHouse™
1663 Liberty Drive
Bloomington, IN 47403
www.authorhouse.com
Phone: 1 (800) 839-8640

© 2018 Johnna Anne Gurr MS, LPC. All rights reserved.

No part of this book may be reproduced, stored in a retrieval system, or transmitted by any means without the written permission of the author.

The individuals named in the given case studies are based on actual interviews however the persons interviewed portray a fictional composite personality. The dialogue is a representation of the client's actual cited words and entirely the author's creation. Utmost care has been given to maintain confidentiality by altering actual names, places, personal characteristics. Any alliance to a particular person is not intended and purely coincidental.

Published by AuthorHouse 01/19/2018

ISBN: 978-1-5462-1823-4 (sc)
ISBN: 978-1-5462-1822-7 (hc)
ISBN: 978-1-5462-1824-1 (e)

Library of Congress Control Number: 2017917900

Print information available on the last page.

Any people depicted in stock imagery provided by Thinkstock are models, and such images are being used for illustrative purposes only.
Certain stock imagery © Thinkstock.

This book is printed on acid-free paper.

Because of the dynamic nature of the Internet, any web addresses or links contained in this book may have changed since publication and may no longer be valid. The views expressed in this work are solely those of the author and do not necessarily reflect the views of the publisher, and the publisher hereby disclaims any responsibility for them.

Revised Standard Version of the Bible, copyright © 1946, 1952, and 1971 the Division of Christian Education of the National Council of the Churches of Christ in the United States of America. Used by permission. All rights reserved.

Quotations cited from the compilation by John Cook, Book of Positive Quotations 2nd Edition. Fairview Press, Minnesota. 1993.
The New Oxford Annotated Bible, Revised Standard Version. Oxford University Press, 1977.

*I extend warm appreciation to my wonderful family, especially my husband Ron, my daughters, Lauren and Gretchen as well as my supportive sons, Samuel and Jeremy. And a special thank-you to Lauren who gave of her time and talent to edit this book.*

*My love to all of you.*

# EPIGRAPH

Wonderments
Time has given pause
wonderment of life,
ebbing sea,
fallow ground,
foggy haze.
Time has given pause
wonderment of life,
budding rose
pastures green
glorious sun ablaze.

Johnna Anne Gurr

# Contents

Preface .................................................................................. xi
Acknowledgments ............................................................. xiii
Introduction ....................................................................... xv
Author's Note .................................................................... xxi

Chapter 1   Paid In Chocolate ............................................. 1
Chapter 2   So Many Good Choices, But … ....................... 9
Chapter 3   Dandy, The Best Golden Ever ........................ 17
Chapter 4   A 'Green' Rehabilitation Counselor ............... 26
Chapter 5   The "If Only" Lady ......................................... 36
Chapter 6   Where's The Bathroom? ................................. 47
Chapter 7   Trading Places ................................................ 56
Chapter 8   Relocation From South Asia .......................... 64
Chapter 9   Gleaning The Golden Years ........................... 71
Chapter 10  Survival Kit Strategy ...................................... 78
Chapter 11  Get Me To The Wedding On Time! .............. 89
Chapter 12  The More The Merrier .................................. 98
Chapter 13  The Zone ..................................................... 107
Chapter 14  A Chance Encounter .................................... 115
Chapter 15  Jeannette Anne ............................................. 125
Chapter 16  A Night Visitor ............................................ 134
Chapter 17  Stuck With His Keys .................................... 143
Chapter 18  All Nerved Up .............................................. 150
Chapter 19  Figuring The Family Way ............................. 157
Chapter 20  Petticoats And Sidewalks ............................. 165

# Preface

The carriage of the famous roller coaster leaves the station. It begins its ascent. The cart laboriously chugs as it fights the upward climb. A huge bump, a frightening shudder and the coaster falls backward ... Then it rights itself. The coaster summits the crest.

And stops.

The magnificence of panoramic view is an awesome eyeful.

A jerk. The pulling of gears and the carriage lurches forward.

A stalling moment.

Downhill. A speeding rocket ripping into the sky.

Gasps and screams fill the air. The cacophony of lower and upper range of voices. Arms outstretched over heads or holding tight to handles. Some hands cover mouths or the entire face.

The cart stops.

A plethora of responses seen on each face. Astonishment. Horror. Fear. Relief. Incredible bliss.

· · · · · · · · ● · · · · · · · ·

The roller coaster ride equates a life experience. The constancy of the journey evidenced in the rise of dilemma to the free fall of resolution. Each accounting is a blend of angst and recovery to thrill and accomplishment. There is a story to tell.

I have taken a particular interest to understand your story, especially if the ride has become rough. This is not a singular effort but one that is worked in tandem; the even flow of give and take between the client and counselor. My role is to be quick to hear, choosing to fully listen—embracing not solely words but the emphasis, the emotion, the person behind these words. I am ready to fully attend to your personal account offering consistency and deliberate response. Within the counseling privilege there is an honoring and respect for you.

Because this roller coaster of life is shared by all of us.

# ACKNOWLEDGMENTS

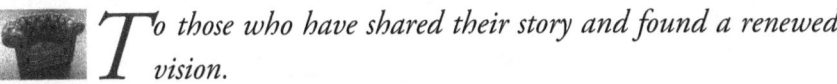*To* those who have shared their story and found a renewed vision.
To those in seat telling their story.
  Finally, to those who have yet to tell their story.

# Introduction

We all have a story to tell.

If you have witnessed the majestic Grand Canyon or sniffed earth's powdery yellow pollen, then you have a story to tell. Some stories have the power to create tingles on our scalp. We sit around a campfire and delight and amaze each other with such sagas. Others may be a bit more ordinary like tiny pebbles happily skipping the wave, perhaps likened to friendly dinner conversation. Then there are the stories where moments of angst present opportunity for growth, that is, provided you really want it.

So as I was saying, we all have stories but some do present life at a steep cliff. Such accountings have many twists that can confuse and bewilder, astound and sadden. Hanging by a finger and peering into the dark abyss, many are fueled to find an answer. As a counselor my job is to respectfully yield to these scenarios—to listen and journey with the story-teller using a bit of insight, a pound of figuring, and a flashlight beam of healthy direction. This is counseling after all; applied theory to actual situation played out with a well-tuned ear. And with a whole lot of trial and hopefully not too much error, a good outcome can be reached.

To reach such an outcome there is a gallery of respected theorists to choose from; their thoughts artfully designed and full of wisdom. I invite many of these approaches—Adler, Freud, Rogers, Frankl, Perls, Ellis, Bandura and Glasser. These are just a few of the multitude of master theorists. In my practice, I have leaned into Cognitive Behavioral methodology and integrate a huge amount from these individuals. As I profile these case studies I will not detail the theory used. Instead, the out workings will incorporate them in practical application.

Theory will fold into the experiential like frothy bubbles into a strong wave. Probability thinking will embrace personal story. And with a goodly amount of time and effort the tsunami will smooth into a sparkling ripple that will woo for awhile until the next rising crest.

But first the story needs to unfold in all its drama and turmoil.

# Continuing Introduction II
## DISM: Derrière In Seat Matters

Your story unfolds in an ordinary office chair; waiting for you to sit and account your situation. Your story matters. As you relate to your families, friends, co-workers and casual acquaintances, portions of history are shared. But sometimes you need a bit more. That is when the counseling relationship comes in. It is an opportunity for you to fully detail your situation to a non-judgmental professional who will journey through the hills and valleys with you. A searchlight will cast it glow on reasonable options that present exciting choices on the game board of life.

To properly unfold your story, welcoming you to a comfortable office environment is priority. Not too warm, not too cold with additional efforts to accommodate by opening windows or offering warm afghans. Modest yet pleasant décor and brightly hung watercolors present a cheerful atmosphere. Quiet and relaxing. Most importantly comfortable seating matters; reducing unnecessary distractions from backaches to crunched derrieres.

My office offers several possibilities. In one corner sits a worn brown leather chair that sinks as arms settle unto the tightly taped rests. I have often considered loading this piece unto a truck and taking it to the neighborhood dump. But the contented smiles and impact on its occupants stall me. There is an oak Windsor chair often seen in old style court rooms. For all I know it could have been its original home. Men usually choose it. Perhaps it helps them maintain control and dominance. Then there is a cherry rocker set in the far corner near to my desk. This chair is fully equipped with back and seat cushion accompanied by a colorful blanket that often snuggles around its occupant. So popular is this seating that one day as I was tidying, I noticed a huge crack right down the middle! There is also the mainstay couch, very soft and comfortable. Some call it a love seat and they're right—once those folds embrace and entice, you are in love!

Finally there is the swivel desk chair which is great for maneuvering about especially when client eye contact is mere inches from me. Most often this is where I stay but not always. Generally I will offer the desk—although some prefer balancing a clip board on their laps—for paperwork completion especially on the initial intake. But at times when the last signature is drying, the client will ease back and settle in. Usually the opposite occurs as the client moves to a more comfortable seat. Since many of us are creatures of habit, their choice of seating doesn't vary from session to session or from year to year. It becomes home, sweet home.

There is a chair end note. While this is my particular manner of counseling, there are other styles; Freud offered the couch, a fellow colleague prefers to stroll with his client on a quiet paved trail and online counselors have no idea what position their clients are in.

## Final Comments
<u>What You Say Matters More</u>

There are many intriguing clients who have graced such simple seating. Over the years of counseling experience, I have had the privilege of meeting wonderful individuals who have stimulated my interest and desire to intervene. These are people who are challenged with life's obstacles and are uncomfortable with current conditions. They are seeking a new road.

People, a lot like me and you. There are those who are fledging, those who are well-seasoned and others somewhere in the middle. They come from varying cultural backgrounds and issues—as well as differing levels of affluence. So many scenarios, but people just the same. These individuals face physical and mental challenges, employment and financial difficulties, age related issues, marital / family status, educational strivings. Once harvesting life's gains, many experience the downward staircase of loss. So many seasons of growth as well as cycles for pruning—laughter intermingled with tears.

I have been honored to offer assistance while employed in rehabilitation work and then as a community college crisis counselor. Volunteer capacities involved assisting at a pregnancy center, senior community outreach, neighborhood soup kitchen and town human service board. I currently maintain a private practice where these past encounters meet the present.

As I detail case studies my hope is to inspire, inform and engage the reader no matter in which chair you are seated. Some individuals in crisis mode may only attend a single session. Others will become regular visitors, a few remaining for several years. However the attendance, the focus is to effectuate change which is seriously hard work completed one step at a time. This is an ongoing process that can be likened to a kernel of anticipation—the seed is sown, watered, fertilized, mounded-up, weeded and bathed in full sun—from which a wonderful bloom is witnessed. In many, not all, of the given case studies, such a bloom is realized.

I have chosen to call these case studies tales. You may wonder why I have done so. Are not tales the engaging subject matter of distant castles and damsels in distress? The stuff bedtime stories are made of? Or perhaps one that tells such stories, the tale-bearer, is spreading around imaginary star dust or idle conversations. Neither. Indeed what is shared is quite true, with a cut and paste here and there. The stories that are presented are full of dramatic flair and engaging scenarios *of what actually happened.* The content of each case is rooted in truth, but details have been adjusted as to maintain confidentiality. A composite of the individual is presented—modifications were made regarding the sex, physical features, grooming, background, location, career, and financial status. Actual names have been changed as well. The given dialogues are fictional but are based on such possible exchange.

Now you may ask, why didn't you choose to secure permission

from selected clients so as to minimize alterations? That is an excellent suggestion. However over the course of thirty years of counseling many of these individuals are living in the fabric of society and cannot be reached. Some have died. Others, when asked, may have been so perplexed they would have moved out of the country. Of course, there would have been some that would have applauded such a request, at least I hope so.

What remains is a human to human encounter that will engage you, dear reader, and prompt you to wonder what will happen next. Will the presented client overcome life's obstacle course or falter? You may hope to see a bouquet of positive outcomes. The reality of such tales is that there can be splendid fairy happy endings; however in the real world there are often reasonable endings that glimpse satisfaction but not perfection. The journey carries on …

My experience in citing these cases, or tales, presents a wealth of understanding as I embrace humanity in each person I meet. The more stories I am privileged to hear, the more humble I become. I realize that such witness has laid claim to my own personal stirrings and desire to change. In the confines of a cozy office a world view is shared that attempts to reconcile life on this planet. We are all so different and all so alike and have many common yearnings. One can feel alone and isolated on a planet of some eight billion people. Or together we can share our stories and encourage one another to make our lives truly meaningful.

We can make this world a better place to live, laugh and smile. A place we can call home.

# Author's Note

You have contacted me, and I have scheduled you in the appointment book. But then you have second thoughts. Can you really share your story with a perfect stranger? After all, it is difficult enough talking to your family and certain close friends about your upset and confusion. There are so many things going on: you have just lost your job, your car is making strange coughing noises, and your doctor found something suspicious on that last x-ray. A dense cloud has settled on your shoulder, and a mist has hindered your vision.

Perhaps an impartial, nonjudgmental viewpoint could really help.

But, you reason, how in the world can you afford this? There are ways. Many insurance companies offer behavioral health services with affordable copay amounts. There is also the option that many helping professionals, including me, offer, and that is the sliding scale. This is an agreed-upon out-of-pocket amount.

Okay, you say, but who can you go see? You can check out various health care professionals, such as a psychiatrist (a medical doctor who can prescribe medications), a clinical psychologist, a licensed clinical social worker, or a licensed professional counselor. Once you find someone with outstanding credentials—possibly networking around town for recommendations—you can call for an appointment. The mental health professional, with his or her own personal style, will lead you through the initial course of paperwork. Generally, this therapist will field concerns and answer questions, initiating the volley. Then you can share your story. This is a critical moment for the counseling relationship. A right fit is needed where you are comfortable with the counselor, the setting, and yourself. Now it's up for you to consider; deciding to simply leave or simply begin.

But you say, "I don't have the time." With all that is going on, you're stretched in too many directions. This is a situation that only you can reconcile. Most of us find time for what we truly have to do while other items fall lower on the priority list. You need to decide that counseling would focus and reset your forward button. Shine the flashlight in the fog to that beam of hope. If this is important to you, then the time can be found.

You will not be disappointed.

# Chapter One

## Paid In Chocolate

This fashioned scenario involves a young woman I will call Ms. Kendal. She was a referral by a colleague; networking can yield results when least expected. Ms. Kendal was struggling to make good decisions, but the roller coaster ride was undoing her. She came to cut and paste and make her life less rocky. Many attempted academic and vocational pursuits faltered. Then she would try another. And another.

Ms. Kendal was upset.

Rightly so. Except there was a silver lining.

· · · · · · · ● · · · · · · ·

I invited Ms. Kendal to my office. With some hesitation, she made an appointment, expressing concern with locality and finances. I assured her that all such logistics would work out. I gave her the address and circled the appointment in my planner.

And then I waited.

Was the door rattling? My eyes skirted between the frosty office picture window and the copper doorknob. Nothing. Just overzealous hoping. It had been three weeks since the appointment with Ms. Kendal was arranged. My usual reminder call had met with no response. But she was quite late, and I was getting restless. Generally when a client was delayed, I busied myself with paperwork or a study on continuing education. But today my attention was caught by the heavy cotton-ball snowflakes loading up my windowpane. Maybe my client was stuck in traffic or decided not to come at all. If she was a little late, then we could still meet and the next appointment would linger in the waiting lounge. But if she was extremely tardy, then we would need to abbreviate the session and promptly arrange for another.

Just how long should one wait? Should I lean into my established fifteen-minute limit and if no excuse rang my cell phone then—

There it was again, that jiggling noise. The door swung open, slamming the knob into the wall.

Ms. Kendal had arrived.

"Sorry I'm so late. My phone doesn't work, and traffic was real bad," she said as she heaved in a well-kept but antiquated Schwinn, crashing it into the side table.

"Good morning, Ms. Kendal. I'm pleased to meet you," I said, catching the toppled potted plant. Determined, Ms. Kendal curbed the bike by the wall, forming a dark puddle that spread like the midwestern finger lakes on the plush carpet. She proceeded to unravel herself, flinging wet snow pellets in my face and on my prized mahogany desk. Off came her soaked red cap—her boyish haircut now matted—thick gloves, blue down parka, and two thick sweaters. She didn't stop there. Perching herself on the straight-back chair, she yanked off mud-crusted boots, which took much heaving and groaning. Completing removal of her cold weather garments, only a bulky multicolored scarf remained. She threw it around her shoulders, letting it awkwardly hang to her tight jogging pants. Easing her lanky form into the rocker, she fluffed her flattened hair.

Ms. Kendal looked up at me, her large hazel eyes expectant.

I smiled and handed her a packet and a clipboard. "Ms. Kendal, here are some papers to complete, and if you have any—"

"Mrs. G., is this really necessary? I don't like answering these kind of questions," she said abruptly, pushing the papers around her lap.

"Yes, this is part of the intake process. Everyone who comes here completes these forms."

I watched her expression fade from testy to resigned. She slid the pen off the clipboard and lowered her head, playing with her hair with one hand and writing with the other. Once she finished, I hoped her inquisitive eyes would meet mine in active discussion.

"I'm done," said Ms. Kendal as she handed me the papers and settled into her seat.

So we began. Words came easy like gentle currents but soon gave way to tumultuous tidal waves. Having departed from a second attempt in college, she was thoroughly frustrated. Ms. Kendal stated that was nothing compared to the last three weeks of her life, which had been "the worst ever." Her boyfriend had a terrible temper that left her stomping out from his apartment. "Good riddance to him!" she exclaimed. Ms. Kendal detailed her wandering from one friend's home to another and how she couldn't trust them anymore.

Unable to complete school, she scouted out cashiering. She had even considered dog walking. Her meager savings were running out, and she needed to do something. Transportation was the old two-wheeler—I certainly knew this!—since she had only borrowed her boyfriend's car. This thirtysomething woman had even tried to make amends with her dysfunctional family, who had disowned her because of her "loose lifestyle." Wiping her moist eyes, she said she didn't need them anyway.

It was a hurricane of upset that whirled about the office. There was so much to consider, so much to reconcile. I said, "Ms. Kendal, if you could change just one thing right now to make your life better, what would you do?"

"I would smack my good-for-nothing boyfriend right in the face!" She raised her fists in the air angrily and then sheepishly smiled. Ms. Kendal took a deep breath. "I guess that's not the answer you wanted to hear. But if I could change something, I would want him to know that I can make it on my own—that I don't need him!"

"And to show him this responsible side, you would—"

"Get a decent place to live so I could I could shower with my favorite soap and sleep on clean sheets. I feel so messy all the time. Then I would find a job. But it's so hard to figure how to have both." She wrapped the scarf securely around her neck.

"Good start," I said. Indeed it was.

We reviewed the essentials, especially a roof over her head. Squatting in friends' homes was strained and not dependable. Ms. Kendal had little to finance her own place. Had she considered all the options? We discussed her parents, but she had crossed them off her list long ago. As we delved further, Ms. Kendal described a kindly aunt who was living alone in a nearby state. She hadn't seen her in a while and felt awkward talking about her. On the other hand, Ms. Kendal fondly remembered family gatherings where she had spent time with this relative. This aunt was most gracious; and the scarf she wore was a gift this woman had hand-crocheted.

"Ms. Kendal, is it possible to work out a living arrangement with your aunt?"

"I don't think so. She lives in another state, and she is my father's sister." There was a long pause. A good pause. She was figuring possibilities, and so was I.

Ms. Kendal was a headstrong young woman, eager to move on in life. Stepping into her thirties, she was seeking a measure of stability and permanence. Of slight build but well-toned, she stood proud even in the worst of predicaments: she wanted her life to change. Ms. Kendal was correct. Finding a decent place to live was priority. I wholeheartedly agreed.

Housing was a dilemma I had seen with other clients. I remember one woman who lived in her car and showered at the gym and another who, while residing with friends, witnessed a murder from the slats of a closet door. One middle-aged man slept on an array of friends' couches and ate at a soup kitchen. Then there was the very down-to-earth young woman who supplemented income by moonlighting in downtown men's clubs.

"Mrs. G, it was mostly my mom who threw me out. My dad went along with her. I like my aunt, but I worry she will be put in the middle of all this. Like I said, she is my father's sister. But … I remember years ago my dad had arranged for summer visits with my aunt. You know, he may get upset but then again he really liked seeing us get along. I think I'll call her. We could talk and see what happens."

"Ms. Kendal, you have considered a possible solution. Let's discuss how you could do this, perhaps try a little role play."

We exchanged roles as the characters of her aunt and father were explored. Our time went swiftly; the keen volley of confusion and pain met a renewed focus that was full of anticipation. Besides being an eye opener for both of us, it was immensely fun.

I glanced at my foot clocks—there are two, situated at the heels of the couch and side table, which fend off looking at my watch. The session had run over. It was time to bring it home with a summation and a bit of homework.

"So Ms. Kendal now that you have your assignment in order; that is to contact your aunt, let's schedule another appointment. I'll write your receipt for your payment."

Avoiding eye contact, Ms. Kendal tucked her head into her chest as she began rummaging through her backpack, strewing clothing everywhere, giving my office a locker room effect. She paused and swiftly hid an object behind her back. "Mrs. G., this is how I'll pay you today," she said as the poorly wrapped item landed heavily in my arms. A decadent swirl of velvety sweetness embraced me.

I was swooning on the inside and was beginning to ooze on the outside. Bold hints of imaginings tugged at my fingertips as I tore through the foil wrapping.

IN GOLDEN WRAP WAS A HUGE BOX OF ASSORTED DARK CHOCOLATES.

Wow! My eyes grew large, hungrily considering my favorite indulgence. But accept such a confection instead of Ben Franklins? This was definitely an unusual form of payment. Was it even ethical? Perhaps I was embracing a kind of pro bono fee—professional work taken on with no monetary compensation—at its best.

Our eyes met. I smiled and winked at her instantly dissolving the uncertainty in her eyes. Ms. Kendal clapped letting the treasured scarf fall to the floor. All was well in Suite 203.

• • • • • • • ● • • • • • • • •

My counseling relationship with Ms. Kendal was unconventional and very challenging. It continued that way for several more appointments. At first, Ms. Kendal wavered in contacting her aunt until one evening, when having no place to stay she wandered around the city waiting for a diner to open. After that distressing night she made the call. Her aunt was thrilled to hear from her and set plans in motion to assist her relocation. Our sessions centered on her inner conflict, the dance of should she or shouldn't she? The focus was to seek out all options, figuring the pros and cons. However the choice was left to Ms. Kendal. During our last session Ms. Kendal sat confident and almost giddy. Yes, she was leaving to stay with her aunt. Not only would there be safe lodging but also positions at newly opened department store as well as opportunities to complete her schooling. Plus her aunt had an old car she was willing to sell to her.

"Things are getting much better," said Ms. Kendal as she shook my hand leaving a folded note in my palm. It was a check paying for the last three appointments. It did not cover the first.

And that was just fine with me.

# ESSENTIAL MATTERS
## *Issues Of Faith*

Often there are a range of questions directed towards me. These presented questions are often expressed like a fox trot as the words are measured and the tone balanced. Other inquires are straight forward in manner, expecting a thorough and prompt reply. Definitely such queries are seeking reasonable answers.

One inquiry in particular concerns matters of faith. Surprisingly this happens quite frequently perhaps due to the uncertainty of our times—declaration of any particular faith stand could damage and malign reputation. Will this viewpoint be received or ridiculed? Being that today's political climate can be equated to the earth's shifting plates; what is acceptable one minute can quickly shift to an oppositional view. It is best to use caution here.

How do clients pose this concern? Mostly by summoning the courage to say, "Are you okay with God?"

To which I say, "God and I get along just fine. How about you?"

Followed by a pause they may say, "Do you believe in Muhammad, or Jesus, or Abraham?"

With a broad smile and friendly arm gesturing I reply, "Yes."

So we begin.

Only those who risk going too far can possibly find out how far one can go.

                                                               T.S. Eliot

# Chapter Two

## So Many Good Choices, But …

In the many years counseling clients, the majority of them have been women. There are a few reasons for this, for one the counseling center I headed attracted more women than men and private practice referrals connected to women. Perhaps I can venture to say that women—pure observation only and no formal research—are more socially inclined to seek professional help. However a goodly amount of men have elected to try the counselee chair and have generally found suitable seating, as well as a bit of self-revelation.

I mention all this in way of introduction of this next client. In seat was a young man in his early thirties who had decided to leave managerial retail work to become a nurse. Initially his focus had been straight and unfettered but as other opportunities enticed him, he became confused and frustrated. His steady wind filled sails so set and determined now drooped. Should he start over?

This is where the story begins.

· · · · · · · · · ● · · · · · · · · ·

Mr. Shane handed me the completed packet as he pushed the swivel chair away from the desk. Surveying the possible seating offerings, his head was moving about like a traffic guard. He hoisted his robust form into the worn leather couch; his well-muscled arms flanked the rests projecting a strong image of an ancient king. His dark eyes gleamed and a huge grin stretched his comely ebony cheeks.

Mr. Shane was dressed in simple summer attire heralding bold orange, yellow and green making his personality pop. His demeanor was ready to fiesta, not a drop of rain to be seen. I quickly scanned his intake pack; general info, no hint of a reason for being here. From his written history there wasn't any mention of a previous counseling experience. Yet, when he called and scheduled this appointment he had sounded dismal. We would be setting out on uncharted waters.

"So we start now", he said in a friendly yet commanding voice.

"Yes. Why don't we begin with why you're here—what brought you to this office today?"

"Well there is so much going on. I want to do the right thing." Mr. Shane looked down at his large hands which he folded neatly into his lap. "I have to say something right away … this is very important to me. Is it okay to really talk about myself? I mean really talk about me and I can only do so if I can do this."

Gently he eased a golden cross from under his tee shirt and with delicate care placed it proudly on his chest. "I am a Christian. I can only speak to you as a person of faith—I hope this is acceptable for you?" His eyes implored mine, hopeful and expectant.

My eyes kindly met his and I nodded. "Definitely. In this office I welcome faith convictions of all kinds. I will do my best to respect your beliefs."

"So you are an Evangelical Christian as well?

"I am a fellow believer in faith and I will do my best to understand and follow you."

Mr. Shane gently caressed his cross. "That is very fine, I'm glad. So I will say that the reason I am here is because I have so many things happening and I'm not sure what to do. I want to do the right thing. It's all whirling around my head like a wind storm."

Mr. Shane detailed his situation with dramatic effect. He was born in the islands but came here as a young boy. With many members of family he had settled in this area and rooted in a gospel church. He was raised with strong family values which he highly esteemed. Once he completed all the required grades in a local high school and graduated with honors, he declined college to help support his family. As a manger in retailing he enjoyed being in charge and meeting people. But he wasn't satisfied. He wanted to really help people so when nurse training came along he pondered and prayed fervently. Mr. Shane believed that God could use him powerfully as a nurse. He took a leap of faith and enrolled. His family was supportive although finances were compromised. However many of his friends cajoled him citing reasons why this was a job for a woman, not a strong man like him. Unwavering, Mr. Shane pressed onward.

Then another distraction presented itself. She was kind and intelligent and smelled like roses. Yes, he had met the woman of his dreams. How? One day studying in the library she sat by him and there she remained. She also was training to become a nurse. He was smitten. The only problem, which actually was a big one, was that she was not interested in church. Mr. Shane paused, wiping his teary eyes with his fingertips.

"Mr, Shane, you have a generous nature and your intent is to be gracious to others especially your lady friend. You care deeply for her, this relationship gladdens you heart. But it also greatly saddens you since your faith is not shared."

"Yes, yes this is so. I want so much for her to see life as I do. If she would only try to understand what I believe but she usually laughs or changes the subject. And there's more. A few weeks ago a visiting pastor came to my church and he was so full of the gospel message. He spoke of his mission down south and the wonderful things being done. As the pastor talked I thought of how I could use my nursing skills and preach as well. Ah, my heart was beating so fast. My bones just wanted to just go there now!" Mr. Shane's hands loudly thumped the arm rests, his face shiny with expectation.

"This pastor's sermon really has touched you."

"Yes, and much, much more. You see, right away I wanted to approach him and sign up. But I hesitated, part of me wanted to wait and see. Spend time and pray. But the other side of me wanted to just pack and go! But I don't want to go alone, I want my woman to come with me. But that's probably too much to ask since she doesn't believe like I do. To come with me I should propose to her … I really would like her to be part of my life. God's vision for me can also be for her." Mr. Shane glanced to the painting clad wall, his eyes distant.

"You're very unsure what to do. Placed in the middle of a tightrope, you're pulled in alternate directions—your hands are getting chafed. With faith you're seeking an answer. You believe that you will be steered the right way. There would be no confusion with this decision for the God you listen to does not want confusion but peace." I watched Mr. Shane's eyes again moisten.

"Yes, this is very true. I will do my homework—if I seek then I will find. I know I will get an answer."

Over the next few weeks Mr. Shane faithfully prayed. He sought out his pastor for spiritual guidance and interviewed with the southern church. He listened to the constant advice from his family and friends. He did not waver in commitment with his girlfriend—one day he boldly proposed to her. She did not respond. All these encounters he brought to the counseling office. Could I tell him what to do? He had experienced a calling to serve. This meant leaving his family, friends, and the woman he loved. His heartstrings were pulled in many directions, but he knew where he needed to be.

Yet Mr. Shane wasn't sure if he had the strength to go forward—pulling up roots and planting them elsewhere. He anguished over these new plans. And what troubled him most was the lack of response from his girlfriend.

On what was to be our last visit, Mr. Shane anchored himself in his favorite chair and wept. He was experiencing visceral aches of the heart, intensely commanding and unyielding.

"Why, Mrs. G. hasn't my girlfriend even tried to talk to me, at least try to work something out? Does she care about me at all?"

He wanted concrete answers for his girlfriend's behavior. I had none. Since I had never met her, I could only conjecture and brainstorm possibilities. And look at the facts. They had dated for several months so it appeared that she had cared for him. They had supported each other through nursing school. They had visited each other's families and embraced cultural differences. The deciding factor appeared to be their dissimilar beliefs—she was not able to negotiate these differences. Over the years I have seen the turmoil of such relationships and also seen those who had smoothed their disparity and blended their viewpoints.

However this was not happening for Mr. Shane.

Mr. Shane's eyes met mine, great sepia puddles that were sad and questioning.

"You need to consider that your girlfriend's lack of response is a response. We have discussed reasons but could it be the most simple, the one staring us in the face?

"And what is that, Ms. G.?"

"She hasn't said no. She may be as heart sick as you and has stepped back to rethink the situation. Mr. Shane when you are seeking answers how does God respond to you?"

The air in the office became still, the moment of quiet embraced us soothingly.

"When I ask God for help sometimes the mountains shake and I hear a shouting in my ear. Pulling me forward. There are other times when I really want something so bad but I feel depressed because I hear "NO!" Then there is the maybe. I don't know right away, I have to persist in my prayer. I have to wait."

"The answer to your prayer will come," I said softly.

"I don't like waiting. But that is what I need to do. I cannot force God to answer me … I cannot force my girlfriend to come with me. This will take some time."

"Yet you have remained steadfast in your prayer so that …"

"Yes, Yes!" Mr. Shane righted his posture his muscled arms waved about. "I have a "YES" to join this mission church and it is very strong, very strong," he said, the joyful gleam once again filled his eyes, indeed his entire demeanor. "I will pack and I will go. I will wait for an answer about my girlfriend. It will all work out." He paused, his effervescent smile returned, his cheeks full and flushed. "For now Ms. G., I have to say good-bye. I will be leaving for this new church very soon and there's a lot to do. I thank-you for all these talks … I will remember you and pray for you. He held out his hand and grasped mine in a tight grip.

Then he was gone.

• • • • • • • ● ● ● ● • • • •

There are many ways clients leave my office. As a team we can plan a launch date and say our encouraging goodbyes, as the client moves forward with anticipation. There are those individuals who depart without a word—generally I see this coming but sometimes I am caught off guard. (This situation can happen to the best of us but if you are like me, you will become highly vigilant so it will not happen again.) There are some clients who may keep in touch by dropping a note, others may call. Those encountering additional challenges might even schedule to return and since I have an open door policy this response is perfectly fine.

Mr. Shane's send off was a promising bon voyage. He had pressed forward and was excited about what he considered to be God's calling for his life. I was glad for him but often wondered how his romantic situation turned out—if he was able to connect with his girlfriend, or if he found someone else. He could have chosen to stay single. These are curiosities and musings that have not been answered. Maybe one day I will run into him at a gas station. Or perhaps an interesting article in the newspaper will catch me up. For now I need to entrust him to God's care.

## ESSENTIAL MATTERS
### Any Minute Now

I'm waiting and waiting. My client should be here by now. The last appointment finished a bit early allowing time for a bite to eat and a quick peek outside. Now I was established in my chair—ready to counsel.

I glanced at my watch as well as the two other clocks that were selectively positioned under end tables. All synchronized—allowing a discretionary glance to note time. He was five minutes late. Not too bad. I slid some professional reading material in front of me, only pretending to read as I checked the door. Ten minutes late. The fashionably late I like to be for parties.

Hm ... it was a good thing that after this gentleman, my roster had a built in half hour break before the next appointment. Now he was fifteen minutes tardy—about the time as a college student I would leave class figuring the professor was a no show. But the phone was ringing and the client was stuck in traffic and would be there in just a few minutes.

He would be really late.

But how late is just too late?

I pushed my reading material aside.

Unfortunately the answer to that is not etched on the Washington Monument. Rather it is more like setting up an office on the seashore. Such protocol is variable among professionals. I am a time conscious person, but if necessary I can be a little less rigid. I can put on a good attitude and be patient. I'm not always good at it—like standing in a long line in a grocery store, arms aching from holding too many canned goods and stomach growling ...

The two o'clock appointment is riding close to my next client which would mean other sessions colliding into one another. The waiting room would have many visitors. Dinner would be late for everyone. And I just remembered that I forgot to take the meat out of the freezer And ...

Just then the door handle jiggled.

Life can only be understood backwards, but it must be lived forwards.

> Søren Kieregaard

# Chapter Three

## Dandy, The Best Golden Ever

Loss. In this scenario you meet a woman who has been faced with losing so much in a relatively short time. Her husband died, her daughters moved a distance away, her home burned down. However she still had her loyal and sensitive Golden Retriever, Dandy. She claimed that he helped her through these tough times. He was her strength, her everything.

But the other day Dandy quietly slipped away …

• • • • • • • ● • • • • • • • •

"It's just that I can't believe it. My Dandy is gone. It's been a month now but it seems like yesterday. Every day I hug his special blanket and fill his water bowl. I keep thinking that he will climb on my lap and give me kisses." Mrs. Jordon grabbed the sleeve of her shirt and dabbed her eyes. She seemed to yawn but a most awful noise came out. In all my years of counseling, I have not heard such a wail. One that starts from way down in the intestines, gathering steam as it hits the lungs and voice box. The yowl was filled with bitter angst and desolation. Her heart was laying in pieces before me.

What should I do? I handed her a handful of tissues. I decided to do the decent thing and gave her the entire box. Then I waited.

Many clients experiencing this kind of loss encounter an intense grief reaction—some more than others. Mrs. Jordon was having a terribly difficult time. I realized this response from our brief preliminary intake on the phone. This woman had lost her dear Golden Retriever, Dandy, a wonderful companion she had enjoyed for almost twelve years. His insides had become cancerous and Mrs. Jordon had cleaned out the bank account to save him, but it didn't work.

When Mrs. Jordon had made this appointment, she was full of recrimination and guilt. In between sobs she claimed she had failed Dandy; there had to be something else she could have done. She wondered how God could have taken her very best friend in the world. He was all she had, her husband had recently died and her two grown daughters now lived in other states. Between sniffles, Mrs. Jordon relayed Dandy's tragic illness and the day he died on her bed. About this time in our conversation we decided to formally meet.

"You know, Mrs. G., I tried hard to make him happy. Whenever he felt a little better, we would visit his favorite park and I would bring his special toys and lots of treats. It seemed like he was getting better but then he had days when he slept a lot and didn't eat much. I sat and stroked his lovely coat and wondered why he could look so good on the outside but be so sick inside. I begged God to give me just a little more time with him … I would do anything; go to church more, give a huge donation. Anything." Mrs. Jordon was strongly negotiating for the life of her beloved friend. If she could have worked out a deal, she would have.

Mrs. Jordon plied a tissue to her nose and snorted. She grabbed a few more and then hurled the box against the wall. Her steady pacing in the rocker upgraded to a frantic level. I was afraid that she would slingshot herself right out the picture window.

Her face contorted and she growled a scary primal noise.

Anger. I would say this woman was stoking her inner furnace pretty darn good. Part of me wanted to hide in the vacuum cleaner closet. The other part, the courageous lion side, wanted to deflate this hostile cloud and wrap her in a fuzzy comforter. I hoped such a release would eventually calm her so we could talk.

Mrs. Jordon was definitely encountering strong grief emotions. Such stages of loss have been witnessed and explored by many therapists who have studied the grief experience. In my practice, I have noted many of them; guilt, heartfelt sorrow, bargaining, anger, denial, physical symptoms, depression and resolution planning. These stages do not have a particular order but can happen at any time and any place. Mrs. Jordon was grieving from a sorrow that pierced her very innards. She was overcome with intense sadness and attempts at bargaining were not working. Her beloved pet was no longer in her life, causing an extremely angry response. This upset was throwing Mrs. Jordon into a crazed whirl.

"I love him so, my dear Dandy … did you know his actual name is Dandylion, because he loves to stop and sniff these flowers. The morning he passed away I carried him to the vet's office and tried to find a special place to bury him, somewhere with lots of dandelions. But I ran out of money so they had to …"

Another burst of waterworks came upon Mrs. Jordon and she reached across the table to snatch more tissues. "I just can't seem to understand it, he was getting better and then he went, just like that. It seems this is the story of my life. Six months ago my house burned down. My husband had a heart attack and died and then my older daughter and I had an awful fight. She moved to another state so I'll probably never see her again. And my younger daughter, I have two, you know, she moved away as well. But I still had Dandy and together we were strong …" She wiped the floodtide that was pouring down her cheek.

From her many losses, Mrs. Jordon was rebounding like a wrestler. Life had played too many grief cards too soon and Dandy, well, that felled companion crashed her world. She cared more for this Golden Retriever than her very family—he had given her strength. I had seen this behavior occur with other clients. Many of these individuals gave all they had to their pets even to the point of forgetting their own needs. They would buy the best food, give them part of the bed or at least the living room couch, and when the temperature dipped, dressed them in special attire. Then there's the veterinarian. I have seen people empty entire bank accounts trying to obtain the best medical care. Some even purchased pet insurance which can be quite costly.

Folks certainly love their pets and try to do anything and everything to keep them alive and healthy. But the inevitable hovers ... most people will outlive their dear animal friends unless they adopt a furry creature at age ninety.

Pet years are short and precious. The loss of an animal either by an accident, disease, wandering off or through the process of euthanasia is never easy. The latter choice, euthanasia—meaning the good death—can seem anything but that. Going this merciful route can free an ailing animal from a terrible, painful death but many owners are often left with a boatload of regret and recrimination. These daunting decisions are very hard to make.

At least Mrs. Jordon did not have to make a decision utilizing euthanasia.

"Mrs. G., how long will I feel this awful? Many of my friends tell me it's really no big deal and others refuse to talk about it anymore. Do you think I'm crazy?"

At this point I spent a good part of the session affirming Mrs. Jordon. Telling her that her affections for Dandy were deep, hence the intense bereavement reaction. The negative response received from her friends, while disheartening, is quite normal. Pet loss is not fully embraced by our society which is puzzling since so many people are endeared to their pets. The irritated comment of "just get over it," is often given to the depressed individual. This generally makes matters worse causing the bereaved party to bury their feelings or take a solo flight to mourn. Such responses could lead to despair, severe depression and sometimes even suicide—although I have not witnessed this latter behavior in my practice. Indeed the bond between the owner and the pet, whether the owner is a child, a young adult, or elderly person runs deep. When loss occurs a respectable understanding would be heartily appreciated.

So I was glad Mrs. Jordon was sitting in seat, piles of tissues and all.

"Mrs. G, you haven't told me how long … how long will I feel like this?"

"As long as it takes. There is no special formula for the sadness you feel. I could say that you would be fine in a day or two or possibly a couple of weeks. But I would be lying because I don't know. It's an individual thing—hopefully each day will get a little better."

We discussed ways to assist her intense grief response. Possible options were considered—bereavement group therapy, adopting a new pet, volunteering at an animal shelter. However that she sought counseling and was allowing the tears to flow was the best course of action for now. I validated her feelings, she really wasn't going crazy. I acknowledged her pain and gave her permission to grieve. Mrs. Jordon nodded, sniffed and wiped her eyes. I rose and went over to her side and let my hand rest on her shoulder. Mrs. Jordon grabbed my hand and shook it. "I thank you so much for listening to me, like I said, so many of my friends and even my family doesn't get it."

Mrs. Jordon layered on her winter garb and readied for her drive home. She wasn't about to skip and dance, but her affect was much improved. Before she left she tissued her face removing any remainder of make-up. She looked up at me, pursed her dry cracked lips and smiled. While her eyes were puffed and swollen their blue hue was as clear as the sky. The reflection from the late afternoon sun lent a sparkle to them as well.

"Mrs. G., I'm feeling much better now. I needed that cry. It was really helpful talking to you about everything. I felt like I was carrying around a huge boulder and now it's gone."

"Yes, Mrs. Jordon, you appear to be composed. You'll probably still have times when you're sad, it will come and go like an uninvited guest."

We discussed the importance of surrounding herself with people who would understand and not belittle her situation. There were not many possibilities, but we came up with two individuals, a niece and a childhood friend. I also encouraged her to schedule another appointment.

Something was present that wasn't seen before ... there had been such despair, such upset but now there was hope. The storm had lifted.

• • • • • • • • • • • • • • • • • •

Mrs. Jordon visited my office several times over a period of four months. Besides the passing of her dear canine friend, we discussed other losses as well—her deceased husband, estranged daughters, the family home. But most distressing was losing her special Golden Retriever. She often spoke of meeting Dandy again in pet heaven. There is limited research on such beliefs, I could not concur with her, but she found these thoughts soothing. As the weeks went by, Mrs. Jordon claimed that each day was a little better, a bit brighter. She figured what had helped, besides time and our frequent visits, was that she had started classes at a community college. This was something she had always wanted to do. She was also volunteering at an animal rescue and was considering adopting another Golden whose owner had recently died. She was excited because she believed this dog was right for her since they had one essential thing in common—loss.

So ended our office visits, although from time to time I have seen her at a nearby dog park, happily walking her new friend.

# ESSENTIAL MATTERS
## On Hope

I watch my client as he comes in. His gait is deliberate and slow; I wonder if he will make it to his usual leather seat. Posture slumps like the baseball player who struck out too many times. Clothing is disheveled; quite possibly an elephant stepped on them before he dressed, if he had even changed at all. His face has lost its countenance—eyes are recessed and the natural arch in his cheek sags like soft clay. His holds his mouth tight. Upon greeting him, he grunts "Yep."

There is absolutely no eye contact or positive body language. It is heartening that he had the strength to come here at all. I am concerned about his overall well-being and would like to see a little improvement before he leaves today. These behaviors may be present in depression, extreme fatigue, a physical aliment, to name a few. Underscoring such maladies there is a key ingredient missing. An ingredient this client needs to glimpse today.

Hope.

Hope can be an anchor for our innermost being. This metaphor relating hope to an anchor lends a pictorial of a heavy ship at sea that is positioned and steadied by such a piece of heavy metal. The skies burst open with their fury as thunder pounds and lightning flashes. The huge deluge from the heavens gusts and smashes. Turbulent waters are raging, peaking in high drifts then casting into deep troughs. But the ship remains. Once the clouds depart the ship can haul up the sea anchor and set its course forward, single-minded in destination.

The bow plows onward to fresh possibilities and ambitions. No rogue wave or hypnotic doldrums can deter this fervent aspiration. Once the ship finds that distant land there is a celebratory moment and then onward to another shore!

Such hope is that anticipation that fuels our dreams and puts wind in the sails. Indeed hope does anchor our lives, and once the anchor has established us, it can be lifted so we embark on desired endeavors.

So we can find success and satisfaction in all our days.

I believe we are solely responsible for our choices, and we have to accept the consequences of every deed, word and thought throughout our lifetime.

> Elisabeth Kubler-Ross

# Chapter Four

## A 'Green' Rehabilitation Counselor

Hoarding is an intriguing topic that nowadays dominates the media making it into dinner conversation. There was a time when people were guarded and spoke about it in hushed tones. Yet hoarding is a behavior that is affecting more and more of us and is not veiled but wide open on display.

Introduced is a client named Ms. Dee who lives alone—with a bevy of feline friends—in slum city housing. For many reasons she remained unemployed and collects a monthly disability check. Much of her time is spent crocheting and sipping coffee in a booth at a fast food restaurant. The rest of day she gathers trash for her apartment from every nook and granny in the city. Our two worlds would never have met had it not been for my boss—I was employed as a rehabilitation counselor at the time. As this agency was working with the city, he approached me and detailed the case in part, citing an eviction was pending if Ms. Dee did not comply. What my boss did not tell me was the totality of the 'why' of this eviction. I soon found out.

· · · · · · · ● · · · · · · ·

The supervisor told me to do it. Immediately. I was like an over eager Collie but I aimed to please even if I had no idea what I was getting into. My case load of handicapped clients was matching Mt.

*Paid in Chocolate*

McKinley but I had agreed to one more. Ms. Dee, who was in her forties, was mentally challenged, unable to work and preferred to keep to herself. The intake report showed no family or supportive folk in her life. Ms. Dee was pretty much a loner. Her days were filled with drinking coffee, crocheting, and collecting oddities around town.

With her disability check she managed an efficiency apartment, well, almost. That was the problem. For some reason Ms. Dee's residency was in jeopardy. A correction was necessary or she would be out on the street or in a shelter. My job was to situate this client so she could maintain her place.

I reviewed the list my boss had handed me and made my first stop the grocery store. On the conveyor belt, I piled boxes of huge black bags, disinfectant and yellow plastic gloves. Grimacing I carried it all out of the store.

It seemed that my supervisor knew something I didn't.

Armed with the bag of supplies, I and went looking for Ms. Dee's place. Since she didn't have a phone, I hoped I would bless out and find her at home. I had ventured out quite early before she left for the nearest fast food eatery. Around and around the streets I drove until I finally found the dilapidated brownstone deep within the city. Although the day promised ample sun, the lighted apartment sign still blinked at me. I had found the right place. I hunted for a parking space wondering why a number of men were gulping from brown bags this early in the morning. Maybe they hadn't finished partying or this was their liquid breakfast. Casting a wary glance behind my back, I hustled to the entrance.

When I entered the rooming house my entire respiratory system was assaulted. Heavy vapors of beer, onions and urine were in the air, glued to the ceiling and now clung in my throat. My loafer clad feet stepped forward but my brain screamed—get out of here! However the thought of my supervisor's rolling eyes, something like Rodney

Dangerfield (remember him?) propelled me forward. I was deep in the recesses of the building but still had a way to go.

The walls were dingy and cracked boasting various scripts of obscenities and bizarre poetry. On one side of the corridor was an attempt at a Jason Pollock painting with splashes of erratic color thrown erratically. The artist was either quite modern or had gone a little crazy. But I wasn't a decent critic since the only light was a single bulb hanging precariously from the ceiling. As I turned the corner, I caught whiff of a new array of smells; stale cigar smoke, burnt tomato sauce and the worst offender, diarrhea. This place had to be the eighth wonder of the world.

Finally I saw the number 213. The decayed brass placard hung lopsidedly on an industrial green door. The olive paint seemed fairly fresh but since the door had not been scraped first, it accented grossly long peels. There was no knocker or bell. I banged my knuckles hard on the wood door, hoping to not get a splinter. The sound reverberated off the walls of the tight corridor. Doors opened and bleary eyes ogled me. Great. No answer. I adjusted the collar on my dark suit—I had wanted to look professional—and tried again. Still no answer. Perhaps it was time to leave. I would have liked that a lot. I would tell my boss that I had made an attempt and he would have to …

The door flew open.

I fell into the apartment.

There stood a bone thin woman with matted coarse grey hair that covered her face falling limply about her shoulders. Ms. Dee. With one hand she tossed a strand aside revealing beady black eyes, eyes that were not happy to see me.

"Hello," I said extending my hand. "I'm Ms. G. and I would …"

"Yeah, just come in, why don't you? You must be that lady the city was talking about. Nothing like letting a person know when you're coming, but you rude people just show up. Well, there's talk about eviction but I've got nothing to say about that."

I followed her into the dungeon like room, tripping over stuff. Lots of stuff. The place seemed airless and I felt as if every last bit of oxygen was being vacuumed from my lungs. I was caught in a bouquet of some of the worse smells ever, more intense than the hallway. I couldn't discriminate them all except for the stale cigarette and cigar smoke. And possibly cat litter. The stench cloaked everything in the room and I feared I would be next. Disgusting. There was only one window. It was slammed tight and decorated with a yellowed set of haphazardly hung blinds. A sliver of light came from a desk lamp that was attached to a nearby folding chair. Disorientated, I stepped on a pillow—or was it a cat?—and fell into musty clothing, my hand resting in a plate of cold lasagna. At least I thought was. When I looked up, Ms. Dee was smirking at me.

She was standing between two leaning towers holding two stray cats. Furniture? I blinked and gasped. Stacked in the towers was every newspaper and magazine known to the printing world. The small woman then stood on a shorter mound of aged papers and raised her arms looking like a scary apparition.

"Hey, be more careful! You've messed up my favorite pile of *Woman's Day*. Now I will never find that article I was saving!"

I opened my mouth to say something and hesitated. A clothes hanger was scratching through my brand new nylons. I sighed. Ms. Dee was not a typical person pending eviction. She wasn't gathering a few things as I had been led to believe. This woman was not a simple collector—she was a big time hoarder.

"Well, say something! You come in unannounced and knock over my things. Look you even kicked my wonderful afghans I made to keep my cats warm! You could at least pick them up."

"Ms. Dee, that's why I'm here, to help cleanup. You have so much clutter the landlord wants to evict you. So if we could throw a few things away …"

"Away! I should say not! You're going in the dumpster!"

"We don't have to throw everything out, maybe some things like the rotten food over here and all those cigarette butts. You don't want to attract animals—that would be unhealthy for you."

Just then a large furry creature ran over my shoes and under a nearby stack. My cropped hair stood straight up. That was no feline pet. But with all these cats around, how could these rodents survive? I had no idea and all this thinking was giving me a migraine—it was time to get to work. I grabbed a black bag and crammed it full.

"My treasures, my treasures! You can't do this. You're lying. Those people can't put my stuff on the street. This is a free country and they're taking my life away from me." The deeply lined face twisted in anger as she shook her fist toward the Town Hall. She crumpled to the floor and wailed. In moments six cats surrounded her. One jumped into her lap and two others hugged her shoulder.

Her odd moaning was unnerving—unearthly and ghostly.

I had to admit that Ms. Dee was right about the violation since I had forgotten to hand her the warning notice. Yes, it's a free country until a peculiar brand of living infringes on others. Seeing that rat was all I needed. I dug the envelope from my jacket pocket and handed it to her. Ms. Dee grabbed the paper and rooted for her thick eye glasses. Incredibly she plunged her hand down somewhere in a pile and pulled out purple bifocals. She perched them on her nose.

I plopped the black bag down and waited.

And waited. The wailing had eased up, but what came next was quite unbelievable. Upon reading the letter, Ms. Dee tore it to shreds while making a strange clucking sound with her mouth. She grabbed the bag from me and began an odd whirling dance as she swept a combination of rotten food stuffs, books and soiled clothing into it. She filled another and another. She was getting way ahead of me and I consider myself a kind of cleaning machine. Ms. Dee arranged enough of her prized possessions against the wall so there was ample walking space. I decided to clear the tiny kitchenette and make the counter tops glow. The wooden table was next. I pitched old condiments and stale bread and then began scrubbing. I had brought a small lemon polish so I buffed it to a wonderful shine. I wiped the sweat from my eyebrow and checked my watch. We were done. It had taken exactly three hours and thirteen minutes.

I stepped back and surveyed the room. It was still dingy but a lot more spacious. You could actually walk about without killing yourself. The sole window had been thrown open and cooling breezes now mixed with the antiseptic cleaners. It wasn't the Hilton but it wasn't bad at all. I looked over at Ms. Dee who was throwing the filled bags in a corner of the room.

"Don't put them there. We need to take them out to the curb for the bulk trash people." I looked over at the slight figure who stood perfectly still like a performing mime.

I threw a bag over my shoulder Santa style and headed out of the apartment down the tight corridor. I peeked over my shoulder and saw the tiny woman yanking two heavy bags, one in each hand. We worked in silence as we had the entire time, me huffing and puffing while she make that clucking sound with her tongue smacking her teeth.

As the last black bag crested the pile, Ms. Dee gave me a cold stare and finally spoke.

"Get out of here!" She stormed back into the Brownstone.

Mission accomplished. At least I had thought so.

· · · · · · · ● · · · · · · · · · ·

About a month or so later, my boss perched over my desk, his left eyebrow raised as it usually did before the gavel falls. My mouth went dry. This would be a good time to take lunch.

"Ms. G. are you aware of the fact that your little friend downtown got evicted?"

I nodded no but I was about to find out.

"Well, a hot plate overheated causing a mini bon fire. When the fireman arrived they couldn't even get into the place because there was so much junk heaved against the door."

"Is Ms. Dee okay?"

"Well that all depends by what you mean by okay. She didn't get hurt, but her apartment was pretty messed up. Luckily the fire was contained to her unit."

"I had better find her and help her look for another place and …"

"Not necessary. There are people down town taking charge of this case. So you're off the hook."

"But I should do something—after all she was my assignment."

"Hey, you did your best. The bottom line is that you were only a band-aid because she didn't want to change. You can't walk in and change someone, so that's that."

After the boss left, I sat at my desk tapping a pencil on a water glass. I figured he was right—I couldn't alter this woman's behavior. After all that would be her decision. But somehow I still felt responsible. There must have been something more I could have done to help her. What was it? She was a big time hoarder and her behavior is difficult to correct. More research is needed to figure it out. So what could I have done? I recounted that day, taking in the terrible conditions especially Ms. Dee's unit. I saw myself cleaning, sweeping and trudging bag after bag to the curb. I was a sweaty mess and my good suit was ruined.

I had done everything and I could walk away.

Wrong.

There was one thing forgotten, I was ashamed to admit it to myself. But the facts are facts. I had committed the worst offense directed at counseling and at myself, a supposed professional. I had forgotten her—the little odd lady with beady eyes. I went about my marching orders with the wrecking ball and paid no mind to her, why we had barely exchanged any conversation at all. Ms. Dee had become an assignment to complete so as to impress the boss. I had disregarded her totally. Respect was lacking evidenced by the minimal eye contact given. Worst of all I had not listened to her. Perhaps if I had just heard her out, she would not be homeless today.

I had failed.

But I had also succeeded. Realizing this limitation—although humbling—will hopefully prompt me to do better. I cannot say empathy alone would have altered her hoarding behavior, but some validation may have helped Ms. Dee make a small change on her own. Perhaps I could have better understood her rational for hoarding. I had missed out on an opportunity because I was too stuck in knee high self pride.

I tapped the yellow pencil one last time and took a deep breath. If I had looked back, even for a second, I might have seen her as a person. But this lesson had given me new insight. I had learned a great deal about hoarding and I hope one day to be a piece of the solution. Next time I will do better.

## ESSENTIAL MATTERS
*Homework Is For Kids*

Yes, homework is for kids. But it goes for adults as well. What happens in a school classroom session, in say an hour or so a day, pales to the amount of time that student will spent involved in sports, drama club, cleaning their bedroom. The same goes for the client in my office—there is that same hour spent in chair; but about once a week. For both situations that figures hours and hours of time engrossed in other activities.

I am a believer in the concept of practice makes perfect; this repeated action yields a behavior that forms an individual. The time invested to acquire this new way of being was a decision aptly considered and acted upon. Such determined focus can create individual success. So the student that learns his lessons well will hopefully embrace a promising future.

The same goes for the client in my office. The counseling process that begins with a secured trust between the individual and counselor can light the fuse and create "Aha!" moments. Such a break-through can spark a desire to change. But this spark requires continued effort to become a honed habit. This effort is seen in the completion of homework which I kindly bestow on clients. The more the individual embraces the in office "work" sent "home", the quicker the results.

Kindly, I say, since such assignments are not directives but suggestions. Perhaps, I will suggest that you, as a disgruntled employee, be resourceful and seek out other employment, or if romance is lacking in your marriage, plan a lovely evening out just for two.

The suggestions are offered.

You can say "yes" and do the rest.

Most folks are about as happy as they make up their minds to be.

Abraham Lincoln

# Chapter Five

## The "If Only" Lady

Anxiety. This place of constant uneasiness is a presenting feature in many clients and also for the population at large. There are many conditions attached but it is often the common denominator. Generally the feared situation entangles with this uneasiness. Anxiety anticipates the impending event—the could have and would have and should have possibilities. This fuels the internal earthquake of uncertainty whether conjectured or real, often discouraging a worthwhile response. Anxiety over examines possibilities that the stallion might charge whereas fear realizes the wild stallion is about to charge. Such consternation causes much angst and indecision. Every step painfully taken often wishes to be rewound and done over.

Such it was with this next client. Reclining on the plushy couch, with the side pillows cushioning her arms, was a middle aged woman whose eyes twitched and body jerked. Her hands were in constant motion that if it were fifty years ago I would have handed her a cigarette and scrambled to light it. She recounted event after event in her life, each likened to a balloon engorged with scenarios of eminent danger that rose and rose until its stretched seams burst helium. What brought her here today she was certain would be the end of her.

"Ms. G. I came to see you because a friend of mine knows you and recommended that I make an appointment. She said she cares about me but I talk to her a lot and I think she's getting sick of me. I wasn't going to come because I've had counseling before and it didn't work. But things are out of control almost as bad as when I was in college and I lived in this house where in exchange for rent I had to clean bathrooms, paint walls and tend the flower gardens. I don't know how I even finished school. There was so much to do, I was afraid that if I didn't keep going I wouldn't make it. This was almost as bad as when I began my first teaching job with middle school students—have you any idea what that was like? I should have become a dentist. It would have definitely been better pay and the patients don't say much. Then there was the time when my Dad got sick and I didn't help him enough …" Ms. Chain took a deep breath. Her lovely gray eyes now cradled dark circles and deep lines.

"And today there's something in particular on your mind," I said, jumping into the extreme double-dutch marathon.

"Yes, I'm divorcing my husband. It has been a tough time but the process is pretty much final … I just want to make sure I get my share of the house so I can move on. Ted and I will have a good start." Ms. Chain worked her long blue polished nails through her beet red hair.

"So, if I'm hearing you right, you want equity as you leave this relationship so that both you and your former husband, Ted, will be able to start over."

Ms. Chain stared at me. "No, that's not right at all. Ted is my new boyfriend not my husband. I want to start over with him. Ted treats me right not like that jerk of a husband who never listened to me. He always wanted to do things his way—I wanted children, he didn't. I wanted a bigger house. He didn't. I just knew if we had these things we would be happy. Instead we fought and fought and he lived downstairs and I lived upstairs. Some marriage. Huh?"

"I apologize for the misunderstanding. You and your former

husband differed in many ways and you were not satisfied with the relationship."

"Yes. If only he had been more willing to change maybe things would have worked out. If only he had been willing to at least have one child or even adopt. Time is going by and I'm getting older, you know, so I need to figure children in my life. I would rather have a natural child, one that is healthy and beautiful and also have a good pregnancy where I don't get sick and the labor is fast and uncomplicated. With a growing family we could find a big house for all of us. Then I would have been happy. But soon Ted and I will have all this. We will say simple vows at the town hall and take a nice honeymoon to Bermuda … where that other one wouldn't take me," said Ms. Chain, with a sly smirk.

"Ms. Chain, you believe that this new relationship will make you happy. You were very discouraged with your first husband and found that you did not share a life vision."

"Now you got that right. And keep calling me Ms. Chain, this is my maiden name that I went back to and I'm going to keep it. My boyfriend, or I should say fiancé, would prefer I change it but I'm done with that. Hey, what if this marriage doesn't' work? Oh, goodness, I really hope that doesn't happen. But I can't keep changing my name."

Ms. Chain then detailed her many conditions for this new marriage. As a couple they would need separate bank accounts because she wanted personal independence and what if he decided to steal from her? She was certain that her first husband had done so. She wanted a large house for raising children, and of course, for entertaining friends. They would have their own children and would try every means and if unsuccessful, then adoption would be considered. The future would truly be full and rewarding.

Then she would be very happy.

· · · · · · · ● · · · · · · ·

## Paid in Chocolate

Over the following weeks Ms. Chain scheduled regular appointments to discuss life possibilities. After each session I assigned homework so what was initiated in the office could be strengthened. A fifty minute session can only jumpstart thought to a newly formed action. A rooted behavior needs focused time and attention. Often Ms. Chain disregarded these assignments.

One day Ms. Chain came in and slumped into the cushions like a crumpled Raggedy Ann doll. She fingered the tassels on the sofa pillow, her hands shaky. "Ms. G., I'm not so good today. Things are just are not right. Remember the last time I told you I thought I was pregnant? Well, I'm not. My husband and I need a lot of help—we may have to try all those methods of getting pregnant. We should just forget it. Adoption isn't any better." She blew her nose and looked down at her feet.

"Ms. Chain, this is discouraging news ... You appear very frustrated with the entire process of having a child. Your homework last week would have helped this situation."

Ms. Chain gazed out the window, lost in thought. "You mean that Ted and I have an after dinner dessert and relax with each other?"

I nodded.

"No we didn't. That would be a real waste of time, we don't get along. He really wants children. And I really don't want them. It's so much hassle trying to get pregnant and deal with those awful doctors. It's very embarrassing. Adoption is even worse; talking with all those stuffy people. It's all very expensive. What if you get a kid that has problems and does mean stuff to us? My husband really wants a kid and has carefully planned how to do this. But what I really want is a bigger house with lots of nice things. That should come first! As you know we have been living in his tight three story condo. You really need more space to have friends and entertain. But my husband had been dragging his feet with house hunting, so I have been working with a realtor and I have found a beautiful place." Ms. Chain righted herself on the couch, her hands boldly gesturing. "It's simply gorgeous. It has huge rooms for entertaining, several bedrooms, porch with a deck, pool and a lovely back yard. I can see us having lovely get-togethers with friends and maybe his work associates. But he doesn't want anything to do with it. He says it's too big and that we can't afford it and adopt children. But if only we had this house we could both be happy."

For a long moment there was silence.

"Ms. Chain, let's go back to when you first came to see me. You had said that you would be happy if you had a husband whose priority would be children and the house was secondary. Your husband does want children and it seems that he wants them very badly—the house is not at the top of his list. Actually he was and still is in agreement with your original wish list."

Ms. Chain looked down at her hands, picking at a fingernail. "I guess I said that, don't really remember. But right now I want the house more, *kids can wait.*"

"It appears to be that you want certain things to be happy and you want your husband to side with your plans. You haven't considered what your husband really wants."

"Well, it would seem to me that he would want these things—the house filled with beautiful furniture and friends to visit ..."

"Right now, he doesn't. He values children more than possessions."

"Huh! So maybe I should just get another divorce, is that what you're saying?"

"Ms. Chain, I hear "if only" from you often. If only you had children, if only you had a big house, if only you had a husband that would give you what you want. You want your husband to always give in to your wishes; but what about understanding his?"

"Well . . . I just want things to be right. I've worked very hard in my life so I deserve some happiness. Hey, if I'm happy, then I suppose we could both be."

I watched Ms. Chain's expression ... a mixture of hopefulness and a smirk of self indulgence. "Happiness. Let's look at this in more detail."

Ms. Chain's cell phone rang. Now I know I smirked. Generally the office protocol is to turn off the cell phone or at least quiet it—unless the matter is an emergency or something close. Ms. Chain glanced at her cell, immediately her posturing became rigid. "Excuse me, the realtor is calling, this situation cannot wait." She went out into the hall, the door slamming behind her.

· · · · · · · · ● · · · · · · · · ·

Perplexed, I went over to the picture window and took in the brilliant colors of fall. Ah, the elusiveness of happiness. What is it, exactly? Researchers all over the globe have studies that correlate data on happiness—many defining the term as the finding of personal life satisfaction. This satisfaction can embrace such desirable items as marital status, family, secure finances and housing, education with resulting employment and lots of room for growth. It is the comfortable dwelling with the chicken in every pot and a car, oops! cars in the driveway. Indeed for some the extrinsic goals of fame, fortune and wealth are most desired while others consider the intrinsic focus, of say, lasting enjoyable relationships. Yet to achieve and enjoy any of these things, one must be truly fit in body and mind so as to commandeer any given situation.

I widened the blinds to catch the golden rays. It seemed to me that these pursuits were always changing depending on which space on the Life board you occupy. If you are young, you may be driven to finish college and marry your girlfriend, if you are middle-aged you want your children to grow up responsibly, if you are nearing senior status, you may want to give it all away and simply live. And for me? My eyes peered out the window and really looked. The mosaic of fall color was brilliant, tickling my creative senses, beckoning me. What would make me happy right now would be a watercolor brush and paper. Better yet would be a positive cap on today's session with Ms. Chain.

• • • • • • • • ● • ● • • • • • • •

Ms. Chain stormed back in. She threw herself into the coach, tossing her upgraded phone into her purse. Her lower lip quivered. "I can't believe this—the realtor just turned me down, something about my husband refusing to discuss the deal. Can you imagine that, the best thing going in our lives and my husband says no?" Giant tears will now gliding down her face creating ruts in her perfect make-up. Grabbing several tissues she dabbed eyes that looked imploringly into mine. "Now what should I do?"

My emerald eyes met hers. "Ms. Chain I don't tell people what to do. But I always encourage choice. Right now you can choose whether to be happy or miserable. It's up to you."

"I don't understand what you mean. Yes, I'm sad or as you said I choose to be miserable, but with all that's happening who wouldn't be?" She righted herself on the coach, a belligerent pout shaping her face.

"Would the house have made you happy … really? Does your new husband satisfy you? Or all the new friends you wish to lavishly entertain making you smile? Would having children bring you gladness? All these months you strove for things that should have made you the most content person alive. But …"

"But I'm terribly unhappy."

I nodded and urged her to continue.

Ms. Chain sat for a long moment and wrung her hands. She coughed, clearing her throat, but the words seem to stick to her tongue. "In these sessions I have been acting like a spoiled brat. I want what I want and if denied I'm downright mean." Her eyes were weepy and held a genuine look of a penitent child whose face was covered in forbidden chocolate cake. "Ms. G. I see what you're saying … I've become sort of a selfish bully, but, but that's the way

I am! I believe I should have good things in life and I suppose that my husband should have the same—but shouldn't he want more for me? After all he took a vow to take care of me."

"And you took a vow to care for him."

Ms. Chain grabbed a tissue and wiped her nose. "But what about the house, shouldn't he be buying me what I want? I'm so upset that realtor turned us down. I could have really cared for my husband in that house!'"

"Hmm, your use of care is very interesting since your husband wasn't so much focused on the house—he wanted children."

Ms. Chain stroked her eyebrow, her eyelashes hardly blinking. "Okay you got me again; I've gone off talking about what I want. Well, you know I guess I really don't care what he wants! You know we haven't been getting along. What I didn't tell you is how we yell and scream at each other. At times we don't talk for days. Sometimes he even goes over to his sister's house.

"I figured such behaviors were happening. The friction between you both has stolen the sweetness from your relationship. There is bitterness and hostility and lots of avoidance."

Ms. Chain nodded for me to continue.

"For things to improve you need to look at change—perhaps one behavior you and your husband could work on together ..."

"CHANGE! Are you kidding? I don't know how to do that and what's more, I really don't care to."

Ms. Chain put her head down and stroked her forehead. Picking up her head, she stared at me, her face wet with tears. Then she threw on her fleece jacket and went out the door.

• • • • • • • ● • • • • • • • •

I was pleased when Ms. Chain called the next day. I had planned to contact her but she got to the phone first. She apologized for her behavior and requested another appointment right away. The following sessions Ms. Chain updated the current situation—that her husband had secured the paperwork to divorce her! She expressed a plethora of emotions dominated by a strong undercurrent of rage. She was defiant and spiteful.

Decisions were made based on economical reasons. Ms. Chain and her husband realized the divorce would be too costly not so much in the actual transaction but in the aftermath; tight finances would leave both parties struggling. Living conditions returned to those of her first marriage—she would live upstairs and he would commandeer the basement turning it into a fully accommodating man cave.

They settled the matter but it was far from satisfying. Ms. Chain stammered as she rallied from what she considered losing a battle. She claimed she would eventually get her way and win the war. A troubled, defiant woman would define our sessions.

However continued assistance was not to be. Attempts at follow-up met only with answering machine messages. I would like to conjecture that while still living under the same roof, their relationship rekindled. But my gut feeling senses marital discord and break up while the quest for happiness continues on. I hope that the spark of self-elucidation she received—realizing her mean spirited temperament and demanding behavior—will someday change her behavior and bring some form of contentment. My door is always open to help Ms. Chain journey on. I believe my part was to plant seeds and begin the process. Perhaps Ms. Chain will find marital support in other ways; through friends, reading a self-help book or even couples' therapy. Maybe she will seek out another therapist. There are many choices to consider.

The rest of the story is up to her.

# ESSENTIAL MATTERS
## On Humor

Humor is humanity's wonderful gift. This comedic moment is certainly a relief as it uses both hemispheres of the brain to help us negotiate life. Humor that results in laughter can help us smooth over the rough plains and soothe both anxiety and stress. It also keeps our respiration in check and lowers blood pressure. Experiencing a robust laugh can even create the flushed glow resulting from physical exercise like my workouts on an elliptical machine. Even a simple chuckle can relax muscle tension and ease pain. Sure, life requires ample attention and focus, but realizing the funny in our foibles and shortcomings can help us live longer and enjoy our time here.

But one might ask, "What place does humor have in the counseling office?" Guiding a person who is treading troubled waters is *serious business*. If the seats were reversed and the counselor laughed at my dilemmas, I would look for another counselor. The professional relationship with a client is a privilege. It can also be delicate in its formation especially when it comes time to create trust.

Humor requires a gentle touch like seasoning with salt and pepper, the right amount at just the right time. Finding the appropriate time begs some insight—as in offering a friendly greeting to a new client to relax and establish him or her.

Humor can also appear serendipitously when the right moment just happens. The bottom line is to not laugh at or make light the client's dilemma. Instead, it may be acceptable *to laugh with* the person since together we are connecting, forming a mutual understanding.

I would recommend that you visit the upside of life. Be open to both the preposterous and the jovial. Allow yourself a chuckle now and then. You won't regret it.

If one advances confidently in the direction of his dreams, and endeavors to live the life which he has imagined, he will meet a success unexpected on common hours.

Henry David Thoreau

# Chapter Six

## Where's The Bathroom?

This essay introduces a young man, Mr. Neube, who was in his mid-twenties. He was a newly enrolled LPN student in the popular community college where I was employed. We first met when I presented a short course on time management to new students as part of the counseling program. He stuck out like a scarecrow in a cornfield. While there were other male students present scattered among the rows of lovely women, his lanky form and spiked tawny hair were definitely attention getting. Yes, his friendly easy going manner and down to earth presence caught the eye of more than one young lady. Yet finding a mate wasn't his reason for returning to school … he was just plain tired of painting houses and wanted to do something else. Maybe nursing was the answer. He wasn't sure but he thought the best way to find out was to try. His zest and pioneering spirit was so galvanizing that he spread this energy everywhere.

But Mr. Neube had his moments.

• • • • • • ● • • • • • • •

Today I was late. A long distance phone call had snagged my time. And of course traffic was bad. I would probably miss the first appointment on my list. As I hurried to unlock my office, a pencil scrawled note taped to the door requested rescheduling. "Maybe that was for the best," I whispered to myself as I hung my raincoat and unpacked my briefcase. At least I could perhaps finish a bit of paper work before the next student.

"Got a minute?" A heavily bearded face with bright green eyes peered around the molding of the door. Then he swung in his full six foot something. "I'm Neube," he said as he held out his hand.

"Good afternoon, Mr. Neube. I'm Ms. G. and yes, I have a minute." Shaking his hand I tried not to stare at the intensity of his hair and eyes. "Welcome to my office, please have a seat," I said pointing to the inviting couch and the metal chair.

"Actually, Ms. G. I was just looking for the bathroom when I saw your name on the door. I really need to … but I have to say that when you visited my class I thought about coming by and well, hello." He fingered stray hairs into his spiky fro. "The other day in the class discussion, I enjoyed your comments about time management. I have already tried some of those things you shared." Mr. Neube shifted his angular form to fit the uncomfortable metal seat, his feet stuck awkwardly before him. Then he chuckled.

"Thanks." I smiled back. I was already enjoying Mr. Neube's grin, his perfectly aligned teeth peeking out of the surrounding facial hairs. "What else did you get from that talk? I could always use feedback."

"Well I realize that I have to establish priorities in my life, sometimes I have to even change them during the day … I guess I like the way you spoke, you made me laugh at myself. Like when you talked about making changes, I often will think about these things after the fact. I know it's going be pretty hard to become a nurse and I will have to let school come first. I suppose that's what I signed up for."

"Getting used to the program takes some time. There's definitely a lot to consider—a heavy course load, tough home work, papers, examinations …"

"Yeah and there's field placement in a medical setting. Then

*Paid in Chocolate*

comes the big test so I can get my license." He scratched his beard and nodded his head. "I just don't know about all this, some days I think WOW, I can do this! Other days my stomach churns and I lose my appetite."

Hmm... the young man before me was expressing keen anxiety but his easy manner belied this. "Right now you're feeling overwhelmed. You're in an uncertain place because you have been pushed out of your comfort zone. This is normal. But if you remember what you said in class the day I spoke—that you're tired of a paintbrush, wood slats and splashing paint all over yourself. You wanted something different, something challenging. And you chose nursing. But I sense there is more to this change then boredom."

Mr. Neube chuckled. "Yeah, you're right. Sometimes I created a Picasso on me! But there's more. I still live home. I had opportunities to stay with friends and even move out of state. But I wanted to help my Mom, since my Dad was very sick. He hasn't been well for years but then they diagnosed him with a serious condition. He went for all the treatments but he got sicker and thinner. He got really depressed. The doctors wanted to keep him in the hospital, but my Mom and I turned the den into a hospital room and brought in nursing care. What Mom couldn't do—like lift him, empty bed pans, make sure he got his meds, I would do."

"Mr. Neube, you put your own life on hold so as to help your parents. You were most accommodating by offering so much help. You gave your all."

"I did. I really care for my Mom and I just couldn't see leaving her with all that—my Dad being so ill and helpless. Besides, I kind of like the nursing thing."

"You felt responsible for your mother and father and especially for your mom. You seem to have a gentle affection for her and you didn't want to let her down."

"I'm the only child and yes, I always got along with Mom, she listened to me. My Dad worked a lot and when we were together we argued."

"Mr. Neube, you were able to talk to your mother and felt she understood you. You were not as close to your father ... perhaps you hoped that by helping him through this time, you might improve your relationship."

Mr. Neube took in a deep breath, his gaze met mine. "You know we used to get along. When I was very young we would play baseball and he never missed any of my games. We also went fishing. When we caught a big one, we would clean it and have a wonderful fish fry." Mr. Neube's smile returned and his hazel eyes gleamed.

"Those were good times and I'm glad you remembered some. You felt accepted by your father and enjoyed his kindness and compassion." I paused and added, "I bet you can still taste and smell that crispy fish."

"That's true." Mr. Neube laughed and raised his arms, folding his hands behind his head. "It was a very special time. But something happened in my teens. He would always tell me what to do but I wouldn't listen. Like my hair, he hated it long but I refused to cut it. But hey, look at me now ... it's short and spiky and we still have problems," he said shrugging his shoulders. "But you know I really love my Dad and in his own way, he loves me."

Mr. Neube's demeanor had changed. There was sadness in his eyes and his mouth hung in a frown.

"You're irritated with your dad but you also have a soft place in your heart for him. Yes, you had desired independence and he wanted obedience—there was a stubborn standoff. Yet he appears to love you in his own way and you care for him."

"Yeah, I do. I wanted to leave but I stayed home to help out. Maybe even be able to speak to him man to man."

"And did you connect with him?"

"Yes and no ... I mean it was real hard to talk with him at all. Some days he didn't even know who I was, other days he was mean and ornery and took it out on me. But then there were the moments when he would get all mushy. Grab my hand and say he was sorry and then talk about the old times."

"Sounds like these moments were unexpected but very important to you—having your father's attention and love."

"Yes and then he died," Mr. Neube said in a whisper.

Silence filled the room. It was a comfortable one, filled with a gentle sorrow, an understanding and tribute to a loved one's passing.

"I'm sad to hear of your father's passing. It seems that you have accepted his death."

"That happened last year and even though things were getting better between us, he was awfully sick. I felt relief when he died but Mom took it hard. I did my best to be there for her. We cleaned out the house and sold it. Then we found a nice apartment that Mom really liked. She's doing well; she has her friends and volunteering to keep her busy. Now it's time for me. When I told her that I wanted to start school, she was all for it. So here I am trying my best …"

Mr. Neube suddenly stood up his sneakers dancing back and forth. He glanced at his watch. "Ms. G. I have to go, I'm late for class. By the way where is the bathroom?"

Walking to the door I pointed down the hall. "It's on your left."

After a quick handshake, Mr. Neube hustled down the corridor and over his shoulder, yelled, "I'll be back, to use this bathroom and see you!"

I knew he would—Mr. Neube became a regular drop-in student.

• • • • • • • ● • • • • • • • •

I hoped Mr. Neube completed his training successfully.

You see, I left for another position. But at times such curiosity can be satisfied. I was to witness an outcome that I could not have expected.

Let me explain. A few years after I found myself struggling with everyday movement; my left hip just wasn't right, causing me to limp.

I pushed through the pain with physical therapy and robust walking but one day I knew—it was time for surgery. I reluctantly acquiesced to the hip replacement, prayed and hoped for the best. Finally the operation was over and I was placed in recovery. Health care staff was working hard to assist me with medication, pillows and kind words. To my right—even though my brain was caught in a drug induced muddle—I noticed one person in particular. He focused on my well-being, speaking with the doctor, gently tucking my sheets. Most professional and caring, I thought. So I mumbled some sort of compliment. He lifted his head and his intense emerald eyes met mine. A strand of golden hair jutted from his surgical hat. He smiled and winked. At least I believe he did. In my twilight awareness I was ushered to a hospital room and nodded out.

Sometime later I remembered my encounter with this green eyed man. But I didn't see him again. Now I cannot be sure he was Mr. Neube, but I honestly think he was. Regardless, he truly embraced excellence in his work.

Such a serendipitous moment—causing me to appreciate and laugh.

You just never know.

# ESSENTIAL MATTERS
## Marriage, Why Not Bother?

The other day a dear friend of mine—whom I will call Emily—overheard a conversation on marriage in the break room. The tone was most heated as opinions were hollered in an angry volley. They were all trying to outdo each other with the worst case scenarios.

"It's so much work and what for?"

"It can cost an arm and a leg. Did you know that just the wedding cake can cost hundreds of dollars!"

"You have to give up so much; the ways you want to do things."

"Yeah, how about managing the bank account, where will all the money go?"

"People cheat all the time. Have a little fun and let it be."

There was more, much more. But at that point Emily had taken lunch to her desk. You see, she had many details to attend to because she was getting married. And she thought, *marriage why not bother?*

Munching on her tuna sandwich, she reviewed the reasons why she was doing this. Of course, thinking about the wedding day was exciting. It was only weeks away. She imagined herself in a lacy gown and her fiancé in his smart tux. The day had been well planned and while they had aimed at frugality she knew it would be wonderful.

Yes, the wedding would be memorable, but she was eagerly looking forward to what came after. Considering everything, she believed having someone to share life with was the real reason. She had been hoping for someone to wake with in the morning and share her days. Making decisions about "our" life was the best part.

In their long walks around the park, she and her fiancé had discussed possible goals, and were optimistic and content. They had an open and honest relationship and while they were stepping the romantic dance, she hoped with trust and respect their love would strengthen and build. Yet she was not naïve, all the good things would grow in time only with hard work. Get through those tough times to the sweet times. The challenges would be there and the risks. After all does anyone fully know what they're getting into?

Probably not. She sipped her coffee, dunked her cookie and laughed. Maybe that is the real reason—marriage was chance to buy a ticket on a roller coaster and enjoy the ride.

Marriage is not just spiritual communion and passionate embraces; marriage is also three meals a day, sharing the workload and remembering to take out the trash.

Dr. Joyce Brothers

# Chapter Seven

## Trading Places

In today's society so much has changed since I was a kid. This is such a cliché, but a true one. It was the time of moms' donning floral aprons and spinning a whirl of cleanliness in the kitchen, scrubbing babies in the bathtub and whipping up the most decadent casseroles. Home was their domain.

Dads' would crown their heads with sharply creased fedora hats and head out in the only family car. Fatigued after a long day working in a blue or white collar capacity, they returned home to those steaming casseroles and screaming children. Finally they would nest in their evening sanctuary couch and position the rabbit ear antennae to the evening news.

That was then.

Now things are different. Women have traded their worn aprons for business suits and rival men in the office. Salary for women may not be commensurate with men but it's getting there. The home front is seeing variant roles—men are chopping onions and the women are taking out the garbage. Child care has noted a change-up with more men pushing strollers and women slipping on fashioned foot wear and heading out the door. Ah, it's a footloose free world, or is it?

The following case study focuses on one such scenario—where the husband has chosen to be the stay-at-home "Dad." His name is Mr. Dustin and he brought to my office a wealth of personal consternation and confusion. For a single hour this small room became a welcome respite from the constancy of his life.

• • • • • • • • • ● • • • • • • • • • •

As usual Mr. Dustin was on time and hurried to the straight back oak chair, his heavy set body just fitting. He took out a thick kerchief—some people still use them—and wiped his flushed, sweaty face.

"Mr. Dustin, this terribly muggy day is very uncomfortable for you. Please have a drink of water." I reached over to grab a plastic cup.

"No, it's not that. Well, I guess it kind of is. I don't like the heat. But today has been such a rough day. I almost didn't get here. Susie and Shawn are staying with the next door neighbor since Jack, who usually watches the girls, had a high school soccer game come up. Thank goodness one of the moms offered him a ride to the game." Mr. Dustin then took the cup and filled it.

"You had a frustrating moment, trying to be in two places at once. As we had spoken before, if you cannot make this appointment please call and we can reschedule."

"I know, I know. And I appreciate that you understand my situation. But I want to be here. This is my time!"

"Mr. Dustin, I realize these sessions have been encouraging to you and despite the roadblocks you still made it here."

"These past few days I felt like I was losing it. I can't seem to get everything done. I thought when Jack and Shawn went back to school and I only had little Susie, who you know is three, things would be easier. But the house is a mess, there is almost nothing clean to wear and suppers are a disaster. Last night I burned the chicken." Mr. Dustin shook his head in dismay.

"You've been overwhelmed with the overload of household tasks and you're disappointed with yourself. But if you remember this past summer you struggled with all three of your children and had your share of challenging days. Sometimes you felt hopeless but you were able to turn things around."

"Yes, things were bad for me last June. But then I was able to figure it out. I know every day I have high expectations and I get pretty upset when things fall apart. You would think that with just one child to watch it would be fine."

"You're very disheartened with this situation. Something has changed this current school year. You're feeling confused and irritated. Could it be that Susie is growing up?"

Mr. Dustin nodded. Susie was a good two year old but now she is demanding, and throws a lot of tantrums. She won't listen to me. She keeps asking for her mother … suddenly I'm the bad guy."

"Your daughter's behavior has bewildered you. You've tried to reason with her but she gives you a deaf ear. You're finding Susie's behavior annoying; always asking for mom. This request makes you feel inadequate and edgy—like you can't do anything right."

"Yeah, especially since my wife and I are having a rough go. She complains all the time. She's always asking me what I did all day. She can't stand a messy house and my dinners are never up to her standard. To top it off, I have all these problems with Susie. I thought I was being a good Dad, taking care of their needs, driving them to school, playing and reading to them. I'm pretty frazzled. I'm even wondering why I agreed to swap roles in the first place." Mr. Dustin swiped the sweat from his brow and looked at me pensively.

"Mr. Dustin, emotionally and physically being a stay at home dad has taken a lot out of you. This arrangement had seemed opportune a year ago when your company relocated down south and your wife found work. Now you're experiencing regret and uncertainty. And not having the support of your wife has really brought you down."

"If only I could talk to her. I feel really alone. As soon as she comes home the kids swarm all over her. They forget about me until it time for bed. Then I'm the bad guy again making sure they are bathed, teeth brushed, well you know, all that stuff. After the kids are finally asleep we both are so tired we collapse into bed."

"You miss the connection you have had with your wife and you feel lost without it. I strongly recommend that you find time for one another."

"I want to but the night flies by and the weekends go the same way. It seems we're drifting from one another. I'm in charge of all the stuff at home while she works and tries to rest on the weekend. I don't seem important to her anymore."

"It seems that you both are so caught up in so many responsibilities that you need to schedule a date with one another."

"A date?" Mr. Dustin shook his head.

"Yes, a date. Since it is difficult to find an evening at home perhaps you can pay a sitter and go out. Find a nice restaurant or coffee shop. Or take a stroll in your favorite park. I would encourage you to put the daily happenings aside and romance her. Set some sparks."

Large brown eyes open in astonishment, Mr. Dustin nodded. You're right, I need to enjoy my wife as I used to, take her by the arm and show her a great evening. You know, we used to do these things before the children came. We fell out of it."

"This is quite a normal occurrence ... couples get caught up in child rearing, household repairs, employment and let the romance falter. But a good marriage depends on maintaining that flame."

"I bet this dating thing will be my homework this week. Right?"

"Yes. I suggest you try your best to plan an evening out. This could be the start of an improved relationship," I said smiling broadly.

"So let's say my wife and I get coffee like once a month, will that make things better?"

"Once a month could help but the more effort you put into your marriage, the better it will become. You see, what you're doing is creating a new behavior and with practice the best outcome can be reached."

"And that behavior would be having my wife talk to me again. Really talk and enjoy one another."

"Exactly. Communication is essential."

Mr. Dustin gave me a thumbs-up sign and quickly noted his homework on his phone. "All set." he said, glancing down on his watch.

"Our session is almost finished but before you go I would like to leave you with a simple way to manage anxiety. If you would like to try, I will lead you in a simple breathing exercise to help relieve tension along with a brief visualization."

Mr. Dustin nodded and settled himself comfortably, taking in the directed slow, deliberate breaths. For the visualization I asked Mr. Dustin to cite a place that relaxes and refreshes him. I would attempt, verbally, and most creatively, to transport him to that place. Most clients generally choose the beach or a lovely day at the park but he surprised me. After a moment of thought, he wished to be away in another state, in a clean, air conditioned hotel with ample couches and pillows. Nurturing a cool beverage, he would find the best seat and read all day!

I chucked to myself artfully describing Mr. Dustin's peaceful place. The hotel room was tidy, the décor manly and simple. A large sofa and matching sitting chair were fashioned with soft pillows of varying sizes. Gentle lighting, footrests, and freshly washed blankets were within reach. Air conditioning was set comfortably and quiet jazz music was playing on the television. Free beverages and snacks were available on the coffee table as well as a complimentary ticket for room service.

As the visualization weaving its imagery ebbed, Mr. Dustin's closed eyes fluttered open and he laughed. "Now that's a place where a guy can really take off his shoes."

I grinned as we completed our session and scheduled the next one.

Several months later, Mr. Dustin visited my office for the last time—he might call again but for now things were good. Life was fine. Just looking at his cheerful grin, clear eyes and calm hands, I knew he was adjusted and happy. Mr. Dustin and his wife were not only romantic, but he said, "She is my best friend." Since full-time work did not suit her and the stay at home stint was overwhelming for him, they made serious changes. He returned to full-time employment while his wife enjoyed a part-time position and tended to the kids. Many of the household chores are now shared, as they appreciate and honor life's endless lists. Nowadays Mr. and Mrs. Dustin often get away to a restaurant and sometimes a special hotel to relax and maybe do more than just read.

## ESSENTIAL MATTERS
*We Are All The Same And All Different*

When I consider the concept of ethnocentrism—the belief that the group one identifies with is the best model for everyone—I realize how short-sighted this kind of thinking actually is. Instead I prefer to embrace two main views of the world; emic and etic. Emic is a concept that regards other groups or cultures with respect and a desire to understand. Etic challenges us to the see the world with global perspective; we are in the same boat. These are welcome viewpoints to appreciate and honor how similar we are rather than different.

So I welcome the entire world in my cozy office. I thoroughly enjoy meeting men and woman from all scopes, nationalities, faiths and viewpoints. The counseling experience not only encourages growth for the clients, I stretch as well. Much can be gained journeying from pain and upheaval to a place of calm and refreshment. I realize that each individual encountered widens my world view and my heart.

Indeed it all comes down to the fact that we all get up in the morning, have our share of daily eats (you may munch on chutney and I on toast and jam) and perform daily tasks until our eyes droop and we head to bed.

Then the next day we do it all over again.

As you go along your road in life, you will, if you aim high enough, also meet resistance ... but no matter how tough the opposition may seem, have courage still—and persevere.

Madeleine Albright

# Chapter Eight

## Relocation From South Asia

"My name is Zahid," he said. He smiled broadly as his eyes locked into mine.

"Is this where I sit?" he asked pointing to the leather couch. I nodded, a bit surprised by his bold manner and eye contact as I had often heard that South Asian men often lower their gaze on women so as a to show respect. In his brief sojourn in this country he had embraced some of our traditions. His positive energy lighted all the nooks and crannies of my office setting a comfortable tone. Although having just met Zahid, I liked him immensely. We were off to a good start.

But the situation was about to change.

* * *

Today there was something terribly wrong. Zahid sat across from me, his face gaunt and sorrowful. Already in seat several minutes he muttered to himself in a combination of English and his native tongue. As a student in a nearby college, he frequently encountered many stressors. He detailed many concerns with school work, finances, friendships and homesickness. Our last visit focused on time management; ways to structure daily tasks more efficiently. But this appointment had been some time ago, three months exactly.

A storm cloud hung over him—there was something going on.

*Paid in Chocolate*

"Zahid, while we have not met in sometime, I can tell you're not yourself today. You appear distracted and troubled which is possibly why you have returned."

Zahid looked up at me and then down at his lap. Then he his postured himself uprightly. "Yes, yes you are quite correct. What is on my mind is that school will be finished soon which means my visa will run out … well, they, that is your government, will give me a little time before I have to return to my country."

"You had mentioned before that this degree was almost finished but that you hoped to go on with your education extending your visa and …"

"I want to but I will need to work for awhile. I like it here and want to stay and become a citizen." Zahid appeared distant as he looked out the picture window.

"Zahid you are worried that your school visa will run out before you can settle in as a US citizen."

"Correct. I had already checked on the particulars for naturalization and it will take some time and money. Unless I were to get a green card. Then I can stay. If I marry someone here I can access that card quickly."

"So you are seriously considering marrying someone here in the States. This is a huge decision and much needs to be considered …"

Zahid shook his head back and forth. "Let me explain. You see, I was married two months ago. She is someone I met in my class who likes me and said she wanted to marry me. We filled out the paperwork and went to the Justice of Peace and that was that."

"Zahid, this is a huge step. You said your woman friend wanted to marry you but I'm concerned that you do not share similar feelings. That you're motive was to remain in this country."

I like this woman, or I should say that I used to like her. That is, she really wanted marriage with full consummation, with me being the one who works and mows the lawn." Zahid stared out the picture window his lips twitching. "Again you are correct, my motive for marriage was a green card, nothing more."

"You're confused and irritated. This is not the outcome you had expected."

"I had figured that we had a nice arrangement. I believe I was honest with her—that we made this arrangement so I could get a green card and stay in the country."

"You were so intent on your interests that you were blind to her motives. That she really cares for you and desired you as a husband."

"I feel so bad about all this. I guess we didn't understand each other and now I am really stuck with this demanding, awful woman. I try to figure it like my country, that this is a kind of arranged marriage my parents would have made. That somehow I can make it work."

"Zahid, you are angry with your decision and feeling very confused and depressed. You say that you want to make it work but you have no desire to do so."

"I am unhappy and very overwhelmed. How could things be so good and be so bad? Here in this country I am getting a fine education. There is food and a place to live. I can go out and about and no one bothers me. There is so much freedom yet I feel like I am trapped like a wild animal. You know, sometimes I think I would be happier back home where outside my front door people are shooting each other."

"Living a peaceful life is important to you. But right now regret and remorse tug at your insides. The decision you made isn't working out and you don't know what to do."

"Yes, and I feel sick in my stomach and I have constant headaches. I am sad for this woman and I don't like that I am hurting her with my behaviors. I am turning into someone I don't like."

"All this upset has made you physically ill. The set of values you were raised with that established good and right behaviors are not matching up with your current decisions. You're disappointed and baffled with your circumstances. The person you used to be has changed into someone that you don't recognize."

"And I can't stand this new person. I want to go back to everything being the way it was. Maybe I made a mistake coming to the United States."

Zahid, you wish you could press a button and go back in time before all this happened. But it did happen. You have embraced unfamiliar behaviors compromising who you are."

"I have really done what you Americans say, "sold out" myself. To get what I thought I wanted—the easy way to stay in America—I have become a deceitful person. I've been so depressed that I have escaped into my music, walking around with earphones. This helped some but it didn't get rid of that feeling that I did something wrong. It won't go away. That's why I came back to see you."

"Guilt. You have felt that tug of conscience that is trying to set things right."

"Yes, this is so. I really want to take responsibility for all this. Maybe I cannot go back in time but I would like to go forward and feel good about myself."

"Your realization is what I call an "Aha," moment. You have felt stuck and full of regret but now you want to move ahead. Zahid, you are ready to shift direction and change your course."

"This is so. I have been looking over my life and trying to understand what I need to do. I feel pulled in many ways. But what I really want is to be happy and not make others depressed." Zahid nodded affirmatively at me, a grin forming.

"You have been considering possible plans that would help you become a good honorable man. Already these thoughts have broken the ropes that have noosed you. Right now I can see the lively glimmer that is Zahid."

"Yes, yes I am feeling much better. But to be really free I have to act on this new plan. I believe I will be honest with this woman I cannot like. I will do what it takes to end this relationship. I will be kind but I will not back down."

"Zahid, then you can go forward to choose the course of life you want."

・・・・・・●・・・・・・

After our last appointment, I did not hear from Zahid for several months. In a brief phone call he claimed he had spoken to his wife, sharing his need to end the relationship. He tried to be as kind as possible. At first this woman gave him a hard time until Zahid declined the green card and made plans to return to his country. "As it turned out," he said, "there was no dual citizenship between the United States and my country."

Zahid went on to say he could not desert his homeland, if he stayed he would never forgive himself. His estranged wife, realizing Zahid was to return home agreed to sign divorce papers. Zahid considered this one of his best decisions. He reconnected with his family and friends. He was also able to embrace his faith. Education was continued in a fine school where he hoped to become lawyer. All was well, not to worry. The image painted by his phone call was one of wholeness and prosperity. I believe his decisions had given him a satisfying life.

## ESSENTIAL MATTERS
### *Just How Old Am I?*

It is often said that we are as old as we want to be. Translating this statement generally means that a younger person will add on extra years while the more mature individual will subtract a few. The twenty-something young adult will suit up and tackle that desired position; the sixty-something will tackle the lawnmower and backyard garden. Both individuals are determined as they focus on meeting their goals and realizing accomplishment.

Sometimes they find success and sometimes not. Our brains and our bodies rally to stay in tune, struggling to stay in sync. The older person challenges his aging body machine, the young adult gears up a mind enticed by partying entanglements.

The bottom line is that at both sides of the spectrum—and in those middle years—there's the drive to achieve and to perform. We want to squeeze those lemons and make the tastiest lemonade. We want our drink to be the biggest and the best—the coldest and the most refreshing. There's much striving to achieve, including thorough planning and scheduling every day. Yet regarding all ages, it would be delightful to find a time to just be and enjoy that frosty lemonade.

My straw is ready.

As the years pile on, you know more but understand less—growing sage furrows on your forehead.

                                  Johnna Anne Gurr

# Chapter Nine

## Gleaning The Golden Years

Mrs. Desmond is soon approaching her seventy-fifth birthday. But in many ways she doesn't look it. She wears her platinum hair in a stylishly short layered look that accents her lovely peach complexion. Her bright blue eyes dance with emotion, a firm determination witnessed in the crystal shine. Her tall frame maintains ample curves and muscle derived not from a gym subscription but from all the 'doings of her days' as she describes her life. There is an air of fitness and certainty she wears boldly like the bright kerchiefs decorating her neck.

That was before she took a personal hiatus.

After several months away, Mrs. Desmond has returned to the counseling chair. Today the sum of her years is making a loud declaration. Deep lines like an artist's pencil etch her face and dark furrows lay under each eye. Her cheekbones sag, dragging lovely contours into a defeated frown. Her gait is compromised by ailing knees, and sighing she lowers herself into the leather seat. Her shoulders seem weighted with cinder blocks and a dense fog replaces the clarity in her eyes. The woman before me appears to be stepping into years a decade or more ahead. She seems to be aging by the minute. It was time to find out why.

• • • • • • • • • • • • • • • • •

"Mrs. Desmond, it is a pleasure seeing you again. I know from our phone call that certain issues have come up. This is your time to say what is on your mind."

Mrs. Desmond turned her head towards the picture window, peering intently at the ample fauna of summer. Her lower lip quivered ever so gently and her eyes glistened with tears. Then a monsoon overtook her and the waterworks streaked her make-up.

I opened a fresh tissue box and left it by her side.

She stared at me, her damp eyes questioning and wanting. "I don't understand what is happening to me. Everything was good so I didn't have to come here ... but now I don't know." Grabbing more tissues, she blew into them noisily.

Mrs. Desmond looked down and kneaded her hands. I nodded and said, "Let's begin with what is causing you to be upset right this moment."

"I don't know what's wrong with me. When I came to see you last time I thought it was because I was depressed with my husband's passing and not seeing my children as much since they had had moved far away." She paused and wiped her cheek.

"Mrs. Desmond you were going through a difficult time. Loss can make you feel many things and you were experiencing depression."

"Yes, you're right ... I felt such heaviness for a long time but each day got a bit better and one morning I got up and felt like everything was okay."

"That was about the time that you stopped visiting the office."

"I thought I was okay. My days were fine, although there were times I would get sad again—like when a song in the grocery store or a line in a movie would get me crying again. But I took you up on some of your suggestions and along with seeing friends I decided to volunteer by reading to children at a nearby library. I'm quite good at it you know." Her eyes sparkled through the tears.

"I'm sure you're a wonderful reader and story teller. Volunteering must give you an interesting youthful perspective."

"You're right! I came home feeling so happy. My appetite improved. I exercised as well which helped me sleep."

"I recall when you last visited you were a having difficulty with eating and sleeping. I'm glad to hear there has been improvement."

"Yes, but things started bothering me again. What really is upsetting is my exercise routine. Some days I can walk two miles and do my stationary bike and other days my muscles are awfully sore; everything seems to hurt so that I have to sit down. Added to all this I'm not sleeping well—I often get up to use the bathroom or because I hear a noise. Then I can't get back to sleep. I feel terribly stiff when I get up and sometimes it lasts all day …"

"Mrs. Desmond have you changed something in your life; perhaps your diet, or have you been taking any medications?" I remembered in our last sessions her physician had suggested prescribed aids to assist appetite and sleep habits. But she was highly resistive and instead chose natural alternatives.

"Well, actually nothing major except I eat more fruits and vegetables but not any new ones. But speaking of medication, I visited my doctor who I've have had for years …" Mrs. Desmond stared ahead, lost in thought.

"And how did your time with the doctor go?"

"I was just wondering. I told him again I was having a hard time sleeping and eating and even about all the aching muscles. I also told him that I often feel incredibly tired."

"And what was your doctor's response?"

"Well at first he mentioned certain medications which of course he knew I wouldn't take. He told me that I needed to eat well, exercise and stay busy. And he said I was fine, just putting on a few years, that's all." Mrs. Desmond paused, her eyes questioning.

"You were disappointed with your doctor's recommendation. You had hoped for more, especially validation of your severe fatigue. When you scheduled that appointment, there was anticipation that the doctor would see something you hadn't and direct you accordingly."

"Yes. I wanted him to support me and suggest ways to help … not necessarily medicine but an alternative to help me feel better."

"Mrs. Desmond, you're feeling disheartened by your physician's response. He failed to see your situation and gave you pat answers."

"He did! I wanted more! I didn't like being brushed aside. I was angry with him. But when I calmed down I felt a bit silly … that I had over-reacted and perhaps there is nothing the matter with me at all."

Silence filled the office.

"But, Mrs. G. if I'm okay how come I feel so badly? Do you think it's just old age or that I'm making all this up?"

"From all you have told me, I believe you're not yourself. How we care for ourselves can play a major role in maintaining wellness. Yet it is important to note physical conditions that could be a leading causes in changing overall health. I am not a doctor but it seems to me that you have been experiencing symptoms that are very real."

"Are you saying that my doctor was wrong?"

"I'm saying that your physician may have missed something. You have been his patient for a long time perhaps you didn't appear to be that sick during the last visit."

Mrs. Desmond stroked her forehead. "You know you may be right. Often my friends will say I look fine even when I'm really sick. I remember the last visit, I wasn't feeling good but I smiled and joked with the doctor."

"But today, Mrs. Desmond, I'll be frank here, you don't look well. I can sense both your physical and emotional pain."

Mrs. Desmond nodded and her determined eyes met mine. "Then I should drop him as my physician and find someone else!"

"Well, yes and no. It may be in your best interests to get a second opinion. You could review findings with your current doctor—he has had a long history with you and perhaps will support new direction."

"So you think would be helpful to get a second opinion and discuss these results with my current doctor. Hopefully combining viewpoints will get me the help I need."

I nodded. "Yes, fresh insight would be most valuable. Of course you can continue to visit me."

Mrs. Desmond smiled, a rosy vigor filled her cheeks. She now had a plan.

• • • • • • • ● • • • • • • • • •

For several months, Mrs. Desmond faithfully kept her counseling appointments. During this time she researched physicians and sought out two opinions. She discussed these findings with her current doctor and came to an agreed diagnosis. Fibromyalgia. Relieved to have pinpointed the problem, Mrs. Desmond was glad to know she hadn't been deluding herself. She was eager to implement treatment which in many ways embraced what she had been doing already—maintaining a healthy diet, rest, exercise, even adding swimming to her schedule. Still resisting medications, she opted instead for nearby message therapy and relaxation techniques she learned in my office.

While this condition continues to be studied to create definitive and solid treatment, Mrs. Desmond had found the encouragement she had been seeking. Knowing physicians stood by and validated her was a breath of relief. Also with the support of family, friends and this worker, she was able to step out into new territory. Mrs. Desmond is now volunteering at the senior center, organizing a book club and a crocheted coverlet ministry.

Mrs. Desmond continues to schedule appointments although further and further apart. Soon she fly on her own.

*Johnna Anne Gurr MS, LPC*

# ESSENTIAL MATTERS
## *Just Dropping By*

I remember times when I was growing up when a magical moment happened. As family we had settled into after supper activities when the doorbell rang and in came out-of-town visitors. We were excited to see relatives turning our mundane evening into a festivity.

This social custom of "dropping by," seems to have had its heyday in years past when people would have time to chat, or borrow a cup of sugar. Perhaps it is played out more in other cultures or in certain age groups. I recently spoke to a woman who resides in elderly housing and is most gregarious. She often leaves her door open so the neighbors can stop by and have a cup of coffee.

Nowadays the closest I have come to this experience has been with students that utilized the drop-in service for counseling. From the corner of my eye I would watch a potential client poke his head in the door—should I or shouldn't I?

I understand this deliberation. A problem has surfaced and the power to do something is within reach. It is decision time. A cyclone hovers over the student, the crisis is escalating. Uncertainty mounds, the individual can barely form syllables on his salty tongue. In mere seconds the choice will be made; to take off or take a seat.

Drop-ins have their own life. Generally this initial contact develops into scheduled slots in my appointment book. At times, following the initial session, the client does not return. The crisis had met with problem solving possibilities and strong resolve. All is tolerable for now—until the next time.

Of course I have to admit that regular appointments with their required paperwork and financial regularity are the meat and potatoes of a counseling practice. These individuals root my common sense and pay the bills. Yet the elusive butterfly behavior of the drop-in leaves me catching my breath and wanting for more.

When you get into a tight place and everything goes against you, 'till it seems as though you could not hold on a minute longer, never give up then, for it is just the place and time the tide will turn.

> Harriet Beecher Stowe

# Chapter Ten

## Survival Kit Strategy

Over the years, especially when employed in a small community college, I assisted many students through personal difficulties and dilemmas. I had a keen desire to help them complete the curriculum and establish their lives. Reviewing the statistical enrollment, even by solely walking the halls, the women outnumbered the men. These determined ladies dominated; eager to achieve a set of skills. Many wanted to be gainfully employed so as to maintain viable households and provide for young children. This often was accomplished without the aid of boyfriends or spouses. They wanted to become reasonably secure and maintain balance in their lives. But frequently the other happened. Pregnancy. Divorce. Court proceedings. Eviction. A major physical illness. There was so much to figure, so many obstacles to overcome. What could they do?

Utilize Survival Kit Strategy.

What exactly is this?

In a nutshell it is the determination to pioneer onward no matter how many blizzards, floods or droughts threaten your existence. There may be moments of faltering but renewed tenacity can strengthen and focus. Eventually survival mentality can morph into stability if you don't give up.

Esperanza, a student at this college, did exactly that. With every apple that was thrown she would cut and sweeten into an edible apple pie. She was forward looking, industrious and focused. To her credit she laughed easily, often enabling her to make supportive friends.

But sometimes you need a little more.

• • • • • • • ● • • • • • • •

One day a young woman dropped by my office.

Her name was Esperanza. She commandeered the straight back oak chair, positioning her petite self upright, smoothing her long black hair. "Mrs. G. I knew you were offering counseling but I didn't come because I was handling things okay. But now my life is of out of control. I started school here last semester because I needed to make more money than only being only a cashier. Several years ago I came here from the islands with my husband. We had a daughter and a son and for awhile everything was fine. My husband found work so we could afford a small apartment and food. We even saved enough money to finish the naturalization process and become citizens here. While the kids were at school, I signed up for lessons to speak and write better English. But now …" Esperanza paused, her eyes misting.

"There's been a major situation that has greatly upset you."

"Yes, my husband left me." Her hands trembled as she held them in her lap.

"I thought at first that something bad happened to him. I even called the police. They really didn't help much at all. Then I called everyone we knew. One of my friends let me borrow her car so I could look around the neighborhood. Nothing. I came up with absolutely nothing … but then he called." She paused and looked up at me.

"Esperanza, what a difficult time you had! You were terrified that something awful had happened to your husband and sent out the troops to find him. When he finally contacted you, it must have been a moment of both irritation and relief."

"Yes, I was very mad! I wanted to hug him as well as slap him!

When he told me he wasn't coming back and that he had a girlfriend in another state, someone he had known for years, I … I hung up on him! I couldn't believe he had hidden this affair from me." Esperanza lifted her leg and slammed her foot.

"You felt as if you had just been kicked in the stomach! You were angry with your husband not only for his sudden departure but because he was involved in another relationship."

"I feel betrayed. I can't believe it. Often I look at the door, waiting for him to come home and then I realize *he isn't coming home.*" The floodgates opened as Esperanza wept.

Handing her a good wad of tissues, there was a quiet pause in our session.

I considered Esperanza's desire to make a good life for her family with the help of her husband. Now she would be shouldering this responsibility alone, taking on child care, personal career training and the added task of bread winner. The husband she had fully trusted had abandoned her. The roof had definitely fallen in.

"What do I do without a husband? My kids search me for answers and I have none to give. My little girl who is in third grade is a sweetheart but she is really sad. My son is almost fourteen and asks the most questions. They both miss their father but my boy is very upset. They look at me to fix our family. I've let them down."

"Esperanza, you're confused with all that is happening and you're being very hard on yourself. You love you children deeply and want the best for them. Your husband's leaving put you in charge. Your children, especially your son, want to know where their father went. Your heart longs to shelter them from more pain. You're conflicted about what to do."

"Yes, that's right. Should I say your father went off with another woman or make up a story about him working far away? I don't want to lie but the truth is very upsetting."

"You're protecting your children so they will not feel this loss intensely. But the hurt and sadness is there. Stating the truth, at least in part, may help. Perhaps you can soften the situation for your daughter. Your son is older and may be able to handle more."

Esperanza twisted a stray hair, lost in thought. "You know that is a good idea. We used to be a tight family, doing things all together with their father. Now they are confused. I'll think about what to say and talk to them, perhaps one at time."

"Please do. You can let me know the outcome the next time we meet."

She nodded. "But one thing is for sure. I am alone. I keep asking myself how come I had not known about this affair? I trusted my husband fully and then he does this. What's wrong with me? It was stupid of me to not see—if I had known. He had been such a good father and husband, very kind and caring.

"Esperanza, you loved and trusted your husband. The two of you came to this country to make a good life. You were very busy trying to make this happen."

"Yes, we did. You know I think I didn't pay as much attention to him; with work, school and the kids and all ... But I loved him and he said he loved me, well I guess he did. I just don't know—this bad situation is probably my fault.

"Esperanza, you're taking all the blame. You may have made mistakes; your husband did as well. As people we are not perfect. To make a loving marriage it takes two strong, committed people who excuse these imperfections. You loved him and it seems that he cared for you but then something changed. He compromised your relationship and hurt you terribly."

"Yes he did!" Tearful tracks etched down Esperanza's cheeks. She pulled a tissue from her pocket and wiped her eyes.

"You feel totally lost and abandoned. What is most distressing is that you did not see this coming."

Esperanza nodded. "Yes, you're right. I was so busy doing so much for him and the kids. I thought we were working hard to make things better for us as a family. That we were a team."

"And now you are on your own managing life. This is a very scary time."

"I wonder about this a lot. I get anxious when I see the bills piling up, and the kids needing shoes and there's little to eat in the refrigerator. At night these thoughts keep me awake. Sometimes I just have to think of what is okay—like our health and that we are all American citizens and for all the good friends we have here."

"Esperanza you have a positive way of looking at life which is helping you reconcile what has happened. An attitude like this can help you begin making new plans."

"I'm still very, very angry with my husband. But I have to go on, especially for the kids' sake. I've been writing notes to myself about what to do."

Esperanza grabbed her purse and rooted for one of these lists. "The way I see it is that I need to survive. So I have to plan the best way. What comes first is keeping my cashier job so that the kids can eat. I want to ask for morning hours at the department store so I can work when the kids are at school. I hope they will arrange this soon. I've already changed my school courses to evenings since a neighbor offered to come over to watch the children. She wants to learn English so to pay her I will do my best to teach her what I know. The times when she cannot come my son is old enough to watch his sister.

Then I think about how we can't stay in this apartment which is not fancy but is too expensive. Well, I have some another friend, one woman in particular. She's an American and very kind to me. She lives alone in a very big house since her husband died and her children moved to other states. She asked me to come stay with her and I would consider this, I mean only until I can get on my own feet." Esperanza then took a long sip from her water bottle, and grinned.

"You certainly have been busy! You're one determined young lady. As you detailed your plans, I sensed creative juices flowing making you feel alive and in charge."

Esperanza's head shook in affirmation. "I just keep on going—my husband used to say I rushed about like a squirrel making sure I had put enough nuts in my cheeks."

A lovely smile flashed across her face, her moist eyes brightened.

"Esperanza, this comment brought a fond memory of your husband."

"Yes, it's just that I had depended on my husband too much. I need to depend on me. I need to be positive and not get so down about all this."

"You have been through a great loss. But you realize that you need to press forward. You believe you can manage especially with your resourceful manner and determined attitude."

Esperanza looked past me to the landscaped watercolor on the far wall, mellow and gentle in perspective. "You know Mrs. G. I am like those trees, being blown about but not falling."

I nodded in agreement.

• • • • • • • • ● • • • • • • • • •

Esperanza arranged appointments for several weeks and attended each one. She was eager to get her plans up and running. With some cutting and pasting, a schedule—which included her children, work, and school— was put in place. It was busy but Esperanza claimed this pace helped her discover a new self and not dwell constantly on the past. However there were days Esperanza grieved the loss her marriage, feeling much guilt and remorse. This cloud of depression dampened her spirit. She yearned for some form of reconciliation. But her husband refused to speak to her. In several sessions we reviewed possibilities and often discussed forgiveness. Could she pardon her husband's actions; not to validate his inappropriate behavior but to be set free? Could she do this without him? Not easy but it could be done. It is optimal to engage the offending party but much of this business can be done on our own. She could also leave behind the constant regret and recrimination. Such choices would release that noose of anger and retaliation and allow her to once again enjoy life.

Esperanza was on her way beyond surviving to thriving.

• • • • • • • • ● • • • • • • • •

Nearing graduation, Esperanza unexpectedly dropped by my office. She had a skip in her gait and a radiant smile spread from dimple to dimple. Her large brown eyes were clear, her face aglow.

"Mrs. G., I came by today to let you know that I am so excited about graduation. You will come?"

"Esperanza, I am very happy for you! It has been such a challenging ride but you managed to finish what you started."

"Yes, I am glad to have made it this far. And Mrs. G, you really helped. When I wasn't sure of anything you believed in me."

"I appreciate the compliment. But I have to add that you did a lot of work. I commend you on your accomplishment. Your children must be very proud of you."

"They are. I'm glad I can be a good provider. I plan to get a real good job and even continue my education."

"You want to go forward. I know you will do well."

"How do you know this Mrs. G.?"

"Now I did my homework and found out what your name really means."

She blushed, a mischievous look dancing on her face. "So you know it means hopeful."

"Exactly. You rose to fully honor your name—you are a woman who is full of hope. And you had the desire to act on it."

Esperanza went on her way. A few days later well wishes were exchanged at the graduation ceremony as she proudly showed me her diploma. As she walked out the door, the maroon gown flowing behind her, I knew it would be the last time I would see Esperanza. But that was okay because I knew she would be alright.

# ESSENTIAL MATTERS
## *Looking At Forgiveness*

One day I asked a friend how many times a person should forgive. "Seventy times seven," she said, having learned this from earlier faith training. That's an awesome number of occasions to forgive suggesting that this given amount was not set in granite, making such a response a well honed habit.

Perhaps it is necessary to back track and consider just what is forgiveness? Essentially it is an action that pardons another for an offense and is then granted mercy. You might say what for? Many would rather elect to run from this concept but some might lean into the store front to get a peak ... and think about it.

Often I suggest this response to my clients. And yes, many disregard its importance. Yet there are those whose innermost beings are quickened by this view but still straddle the fence.

Making such a choice is contrary to the angry pot of emotions stirring within. Consider forgiveness akin to a roll of plastic wrap. All of a sudden the plastic refuses to yield and instead there is much yanking and grunting required just to untangle it. Like the resistive plastic wrap, the given relationship is flawed. Conviction is knocking; the nudge to approach the offender and hopefully settle the matter by reaching a peaceful resolution. This action is very difficult causing you to squirm. You might say something is very wrong. Actually something is very right. You have made that first difficult step. A step based not on feeling but on thoughtful insight. As you struggle to pull smooth the tangled wrap—the estranged relationship— obstacles may get in the way.

There is doubt. Perhaps, you reason, the situation really was not that serious; the offense received was an overreaction. Forgiveness is not necessary at all. Or maybe the circumstance was so severe that the gesture of forgiveness appears oversimplified and flimsy. It is hardly worth the effort.

There is personal inflexibility. Why should you make the first move, after all this breach has caused great personal pain? There is justification to reject forgiveness and instead seek vindication with the accuser. Such vengeance wraps vines of anger and hostility around the heart.

There is embarrassment. Will seeking forgiveness look like weakness or foolishness? Will the party granted forgiveness respond with total disregard and neglect? Perhaps it would be to your advantage keep silent and internalize the matter.

Let's consider the tables are reversed. Say, I wasn't the injured party hoping to confront and reconcile. Instead, I was the offender and I didn't even know it. Or want to know it. But my lifetime friend did. There was a severing in our relationship and she was asking for my forgiveness. At first I did not comply. Then realizing my trespass, I wasn't ready for the forgiveness space. But the injured party was. Her manner was as gentle as a dove and mine was heaving a shield and brandishing a sword. Then came the comment, "I hope we can mend our relationship ... you have been a wonderful friend; I wouldn't want to lose you."

What should I do? My mind screamed no, my body arched in retaliation. But something in me desired to make amends. It was decision time. Putting on forgiveness, the struggle with the errant plastic wrap eased up. Suddenly I was able to untwist it and pull clean even pieces.

Forgiveness. These are some possible responses. The best outcome is for mutual reconciliation to be found—the offended party seeks to reconcile and the offending party offers forgiveness. Optimally for both there is personal change.

A reasonable and wonderful outcome can result in the asking for forgiveness even if the offending party resists and walks away. This step can release the injured person from bitterness and hurt. It is a choice to liberate that strangled hold. But by no means is this response an acceptance of inappropriate behavior; such poor conduct requires adjusting. Instead it is a gesture in mercy, that unearned favor, so that there is a release from vindictiveness and a yield to peace of mind.

Freeing ourselves to become all we could be.

When you learn not to want things so badly,
life comes to you.

> Jessica Lange

# Chapter Eleven

## Get Me To The Wedding On Time!

I was wrapping up in the office when the phone rang. A youthful, kind voice spoke with enlivened diction. Perhaps an English teacher? I noted the essential information that would be later fortified with an intake application. I gathered the usual personal data such as residence, birth date and insurance claims, yet some pieces were missing. Yes, I found she was a heath professional employed in a well known hospital in the area—hmm … not a teacher after all. She did not mention marital status or any relationship difficulties. Her voice carried no hint of melancholy or depression. She was definitely not angry or confused. So what was the presenting issue? Ah, there is limitation in phone consultation—the entire picture can lack clarity (unless I fully utilize electronic services which I do not). Getting to the point I asked this amicable woman the reason for her call. She said, "I just want to talk and your office is easy to get to." There it was, pure honestly, nothing in particular and I was an easy location on the map. I scheduled an appointment for Ms. Lucie—I did get her name—gave her directions and bit about the office layout. Any questions? None. She assured me she was looking forward to the session.

As I noted the appointment, I imagined Ms. Lucie to stand confident and tall with short black hair and a determined gait. I chuckled to myself, this was all pure conjecture. In a few days I would find out for sure.

• • • • • • • • ● • • • • • • • •

The office door swung open and in bounced a petit young woman well dressed in simple summer attire of shorts and matching top. The bold reds and violets went perfect with her shoulder length blonde hair and lavender eyes. Tight muscles and glowing bronze skin radiated health. She grabbed my hand, shook it vigorously and introduced herself.

Ms. Lucie had arrived.

Her very presence danced away the shadows from the room. She eyed the office layout, and bounded over to the rocking chair. Ease of movement blended with exactness of joints and muscles exuded athletic prowess—at least this deduction would prove correct.

Ms.Lucie sat confident, crossing one suntanned leg over the other her hands resting in her lap. She was ready to begin.

Curiosity tapped my shoulder. Could she be as well adjusted as she appeared? Or were there buried secrets that would come pouring out? Perhaps she was in such fine mental health that I was looking at a well visit. Indeed her overall physical health was exemplary, probably due to a combination of good genes and daily self-discipline.

"Good morning Ms. Lucie! I have a packet for you to complete which we can get to in a few minutes." Hmm … I was surprising myself. Generally initial completion of this information is absolutely primary. And for good reason—there are essentials documented that paint a picture of the person seated before me. But today I wished to glean slowly. I placed the application forms on my desk and smiled at Ms. Lucie. "On your way to this office, perhaps you were considering what you wanted to say. If so, let's start there."

"Yes I was actually. I really wanted to tell you about my life. So much is happening … a lot of good stuff. I'm figuring what to do about tennis. I had been playing just for recreation but in the last year I'm becoming more competitive and I'm getting ready to play in a local tournament. I'm so excited!"

"Congratulations to you! All your effort has taken your game to a new level. This is quite an accomplishment."

Yes, I'm proud of myself. Now I need to arrange my work schedule at the hospital. I work as a physical therapist so this can be tricky. I assist recovering orthopedic patients and you never know when it will be slow or crazy. I don't want to let anyone down."

"You are concerned about requesting time off … you're very responsible and want to follow through. Your career is important to you as well as your avid sports interest."

Ms. Lucie shook her head affirmatively. "You're right, I love helping people get back on their feet and be independent again. Tennis is also a wonderful part of my life. I hope my supervisor will adjust the schedule; she is generally fair and accommodating. I plan to meet with her tomorrow and go over all the details. I'm a bit nervous about it but I guess it will work out. Most things do."

"Being unsure about your supervisor's response is normal. You appear to know what you want and how you wish to negotiate the situation. You are level-headed and confident. Those qualities will help you figure this out."

"Yes, you're right; I'm trying to be responsible. This situation should be okay, my supervisor usually is willing to help me. But I'm also worried about finances—if I cut too many hours how will I pay for a new car and my wedding?"

Ms. Lucie was hoping for an answer. While her manner did not exhibit anxiety, her words stated uncertainty. Now we were getting somewhere. This young woman had a strong grasp on life situations—a career, sports and a relationship—but juggling these major life events was taking effort.

"Ms. Lucie, you have a lot of activity going on in your life … a lot to be proud and excited about. You have a satisfying position in physical therapy, you're accomplished in sports and you're in a serious relationship. There are so many happenings, positive stressors which you are attempting to handle."

"That's for sure! But it's hard handling all these positive stressors, as you would say. Friends and family are great. My fiancé is wonderful." She paused, examining a fingernail. "Sometimes getting another opinion helps. That's why I came here. A close friend of mine recommended you—she says you are open-minded on many different issues …"

I nodded, accepting the kind word and waited for Ms. Lucie to continue.

"Well, my fiancé and I get along very well. We have so much in common. We both participate in sports—mine is tennis and his soccer. I enjoy when we cook together and travel places especially to art galleries—because Jim, my fiancé, loves art and works as a commercial artist. But we have some differences. I like going to church but my boyfriend is not interested. He has visited my church but he doesn't want to join. I really want to get married in my parish—my parents were married there. This is a huge problem, because he would rather get married outside in a meadow somewhere." Her countenance changed. The luster is her eyes dimmed and her upper lip quivered.

"Ms. Lucie, I sense this situation greatly troubles you. It appears you have shared many experiences but there is huge conflict regarding the service for your wedding. You have learned a lot from each other but there are some concerns to iron out."

"You're right. I pray a lot and want the best for myself and Jim. He is a very kind man and he is good to me. But there are other issues we don't agree on, like having children and how to raise them. Then I feel hurt. At times he doesn't seem to care about what I think. He has his own opinion about things." Ms. Lucie turned her gaze to a far corner of the room.

"You say that you're hurt—personally offended because your

viewpoints are being pushed away. You're angry because you fiancé has his own views."

"Yeah, I get pretty mad. Our arguing is so irritating. I can't stand it."

"Ms. Lucie, you're actually stepping into what can make a good relationship—or one very difficult one. Such conflicting opinions regarding how to live can offer a huge range of alternatives, choices that can add variety and zest to your relationship. Working out those differences can either break a couple apart or add new dimensions."

"Hmm, I see what you are saying. That if we see everything the same, things could get kind of boring. Having different views can spice up life, which in many ways we already do, but we are very stuck about some issues especially this wedding. I'm not sure what do—this entire situation makes me crazy."

"Ms. Lucie, you're strong-willed which leaves you confused and irritated. May I suggest you look at the concept of compromise. This is a way to resolve differences in coming to a mutual understanding by bending for each other. Generally a union of two people, no matter the actual location, initiates a promise to love and care for each other in the good times as well as the difficult ones. This is a serious promise. It requires seeking the best for one another which often embraces personal sacrifice. Such bending can strengthen the marital bond."

Ms. Lucie spent a long moment tapping her well manicured nails together.

"Well, you got me. I always wanted to walk down a carpeted red aisle elegant in my dress and silky train. But Jim prefers the simple and more causal. He's that kind of guy." She groaned. "But I see what you're getting at. Starting our life making decisions together is important. We're not talking about what to order at the fast food window, we're talking about us."

I smiled. "Exactly. You both have interests and hobbies in common. However you differ not only on the site of your wedding but on basic life goals and values like having children and ways to raise them."

"We probably need to talk about these issues more."

"Yes. Communication is vital. The healthiest relationships are anchored in a value system where both parties are concerned with the well being of the other and willing to sacrifice particular ways so as to form a shared vision. This is compromise at its best."

"So if I'm hearing you right … my fiancé and I need to work on our relationship and find out what is really important in each other's lives. And, as you say, bend a little."

I nodded. "You see life one way; your fiancé is coming from another viewpoint. It appears you have only begun to understand him."

"Yeah, there's a lot of work to do. Sometimes we avoid topics that irritate us and, instead we find a lighter subject. We need to work on these things now, not wait to after we're married. But this is going to be really hard." Ms. Lucie sighed and shook her head.

"I agree this will be hard. Yet the groundwork you establish at this point will carry you into the future." I gave Ms. Lucie a determined look.

"That will mean a lot of time and effort. We are supposed to finish our wedding invitations and finalize our wedding plans. I'm not sure where to start."

"Do you love one another?"

Ms. Lucie nodded her head in affirmation, her eyes wide and questioning.

"If you love one another then you will find a way. I encourage you to seek each other's best interests, go the extra mile for one another and discover fresh possibilities. This will challenge your love for each other and make it stronger or you will realize that it is not time to seal your relationship."

Quiet filled the office. The only sounds were muffled sobs as Ms. Lucie wiped the corners of her eyes.

• • • • • • • ● • • • • • • • •

Ms. Lucie scheduled several more office sessions piecing together new plans. Her fiancé had agreed to postpone the wedding date until they could reconcile their differences. On occasion he visited our sessions and was most supportive.

Ms. Lucie and her fiancé did their homework by examining many issues; honestly discussing their viewpoints and experiences. They agreed to spend more time getting to know one another. Before arranging another wedding date they had a wait and see attitude—making sure they were established and content. Most heartening during this process was their desire to work together. This was a joint effort; forgoing the "I" for the "we".

• • • • • • • ● • • • • • • • •

On a vibrant spring day, a fancy envelope slipped through the office mail slot. A wedding invitation. A short note accompanied it. Ms. Lucie and her fiancé nicely thanked me for the counseling time. They offered me a seat to their wedding which would be held within the elegant marbled walls of a nearby art museum. A Justice of the Peace would officiate.

Smiling, I eased back in my worn office chair. Their words were kind and genuine. Such written sentiments were refreshing. And humbling. After all, they had contributed so much to the counseling process. As to attending the wedding, was this appropriate behavior or conflicting interest for a counselor? I pictured myself dropping tomato sauce on my outfit and then sipping a bit too much champagne. I chuckled and shook my head. They would do just fine without me. But on their wedding day, I will think of them most fondly.

## ESSENTIAL MATTERS
*Finding Kindness In Feathered Friends*

With a growing planet full of wonderful men and women, there would seem to be endless possibilities for developing friendships, embracing romance and even appreciating the next door neighbor who gave you the cup of sugar. You would hope so but sometimes it doesn't happen that way. As the traffic hustles down the highway so do we, rushing about accomplishing endless lists which are quite necessary for survival. There isn't enough time for each other.

I believe we all need a daily hug—that welcoming acknowledgement showing esteem for one another. This hug can be witnessed in the simple things, the kind wink of the sales clerk, an unexpected favor, a supportive phone call or card. And of course receiving that hug in a genuine, loving embrace is the best.

Sometimes it is easier to befriend one of the many furry creatures around us, often dogs or cats. Companionship is found in that give and take relationship of human to furry friend. This companionship provides a healthy bond for support and love, one that allows a sense of connection and happiness for both parties.

That daily hug can be encountered in many ways. And it is important to give and receive as many as you can.

Animals are such agreeable friends—they ask no questions, they pass no criticisms.

George Elliot

# Chapter Twelve

## The More The Merrier

His name was George. He was a middle-aged man sporting wavy salt and pepper hair. He kept himself well, always dressed in clean dress pants and a collared shirt. Of course, he wore highly polished shoes. George provided for himself by working as an accountant in a local company. He lived alone, staying in the same roomy colonial where he had grown up. Sometime ago both parents had died which was a topic of frequent discussion. In our sessions he would often revisit high school days and two buddies who also were deceased. Although an agreeable man, his shy side often hindered making new friends. Yet with a little urging and a lot of patience—which most people are short on these days—conversation with George bloomed especially with his animal stories. You see, he was most comfortable talking to his family of furry creatures—his cats.

George was a pet collector. This behavior wasn't something he planned. It just happened. His first cat was a stray that followed him home and wouldn't leave. That was okay with George. Then the others came. Sometimes they would curl up on his doorstep and refuse to move. (In my backyard I experienced a similar visitation when a huge white cat jumped into my lap and stared at me with his one green and one yellow eye.)

George could not refuse any of them. In our most recent session he disclosed that he had nine house cats. Most of their ages were unknown, but George knew some were getting weak. He could hardly discuss the inevitable—that he would probably outlive all of them. So saddened by this situation, he invited me to visit his home.

• • • • • • • • • ● • • • • • • • • • •

The slate blue colonial sat proudly in the neighborhood. Well manicured trees and shrubs flanked it and the grass had recently mowed diagonal lines. As I lifted the brass knocker, George abruptly swung open the door. His face beamed as he ushered me in. Chuckling, I held out my hand in greeting. "Why George, I hadn't expected such a great welcome!"

"Well, Mrs. G. this is my home and I'm so glad you could come."

"I am honored that you asked me. What a roomy and bright living room you have here!" I meant it. For a man living on his own, I had expected a certain messiness and perhaps a stale smell to pervade. Of course, there should be the musty scent of cats but all I sniffed was the delightful smell of perked coffee.

But something was missing. I had expected to see gray cats and gingers walking around checking this stranger out—me.

"Would you like a cup of hazelnut coffee?" asked George as he led me into his kitchen. "There is also a cheese danish I bought this morning."

"Yes George, I would like a cup black with one teaspoon of sugar and a smidge of that wonderful pastry. Thank-you so much for your hospitality." I was enjoying this home visit … an outreach once frequented now had lapsed in my practice preferring the client come to me. I appreciated getting an actual eye view of daily living. But a bit of caution here—to watch becoming a social visit. I had come to take note of George's cat collection and his concern with their health … but where were these furry creatures?

As if reading my mind George said, "Would you like to meet some of my friends?"

I nodded.

"Come visit Papa, come on, Bitsy, Silver, Boots, Jazzy, Glory and Snickers." In moments, they appeared, seemingly out of nowhere. They circled George, brushing his legs, mewing for his attention. He knelt down and stroked one the color of the chrome on my car. "This is Silver. He's very affectionate and also one of my favorites." That one is Jazzy because all she wants to do is play. And Glory is hiding under the chair. I found her last year on the 4$^{th}$ of July! Bitsy is the small white one over there and Boots has the white and black paws that look like snowshoes. Snickers is the black cat near you. His name was just for fun since I love that candy bar. Hmm we're missing somebody ... I believe he's still upstairs. They don't go to the basement because it has a lot of junk, but they are allowed in the enclosed porch." He pointed to the ample porch located near the kitchen. "That's where they eat and use their litter box." I peeked in noting the large feeding bowls for water and food and the cans of quality meals stacked on makeshift counter. The litter box was situated in the far corner.

"Well, George I can see that you really care for cats, and that they mean a lot to you. In our last visit you mentioned that some were having problems ..."

"Yes, that is correct. Yesterday I brought Cinnamon and Fury to see the vet and they stayed overnight for observation. It's uncertain what's wrong but they're not eating or behaving right. I've got to tell you it's really hard to get them to the vet. You have to use these special crates. Fury was a terror getting into his. I hope they'll be okay and come home soon."

"You miss Cinnamon and Fury and worry about them. You sensed something was the matter and you were wise to seek a veterinarian."

"That is correct. I want them to have long and happy lives. You know that I rescued them. I am feeding my friends the best food and give them treats like catnip. Then there's the cat litter that I am always cleaning out. You see the chair over there? If you look under the padding, the seat and arm rests are all scratched up. I had to invest in a couple of scratching posts."

"George, you certainly are a conscientious pet owner."

He nodded. "But it all costs so much, especially the veterinarian. I don't go all the time since they are healthy and domesticated and most of them hate those visits. But when they get sick …" George's affect changed. His head went down as he swiped a tear. "I don't want to lose any of them."

"You're concerned that one day you'll say goodbye to some of your cat family. You would rather not think about their passing but you worry when they get sick."

"What would I do without them? They're everything to me!" Tearing, George pulled out a white and blue handkerchief and wiped his face.

"You're attached to all of them. It's scary to think that they would leave you."

"Sometimes I think they will live forever but I know better. Some of them may live fourteen to sixteen years and may even live up to twenty years especially since they're domesticated and cared for. But I'm not even sure how old a few of them are. So you're right, they will someday be all gone."

"George you are worried that …"

"They will leave me just like Mom and Dad. You know that I took good care of them. I kept the house clean, shopped, moved the lawn and took them to the doctor. Towards the end I even emptied bed pans. I did so much but when I look back I think of all the things I could have done better—that maybe they would be still alive."

"You feel guilty, that you missed something and it is your fault they died."

"Yes, like when my mother fell because she was so weak from the cancer that was eating her up. The fall made her worse. That day I had gone out to play golf and had left my cousin in charge … if I had been there."

"George, you're blaming yourself for being human. You went out to take a little time for yourself. So you could refresh and better attend to your parents. The fall happened but it was not your fault. You did your best to give your mom comfort and caring. You've been an excellent son."

"But they both died anyway."

"You still feel guilty. But from what you have shared with me you did everything you could. Each time, at the hospice facility, you even kept vigil by their beds until they passed."

"I was very upset about losing Mom. We had enjoyed good talks. Then Dad helped me a lot. He shared about his life and gave me advice about how to live mine. He died a few months later. But they both said they loved me."

"That you were able to exchange these feelings was a gift. Some people never express such affection."

"Yes, yes, you're right. I loved them as well and I'm not always sad. It's not always the bad stuff I think about. Although they both died twelve years ago I can still see their faces, smiling at me over the dinner table."

"Memories, George, of those times are a special privilege. They can warm our hearts and bring comfort."

"I believe one day I will see them again like it says in the Bible. For now I have all my wonderful cats." George beckoned to several of his feline friends. In seconds they encircled him, mewing and brushing his legs. One bounced into his lap. George laughed. "I forgot to tell you about the most recent addition to our family. Her name is Marbles," he said, stroking the sleek hair. "She got that name because her eyes are like giant green marbles."

I nodded. "All these wonderful furry friends have helped you through the loss of your parents. They certainly make you smile."

"Yes, my cats have filled this house will joy," he said with a huge grin.

"Enjoy them while you can and make good memories." As I

gently patted Marbles I noticed the time. "George I have to go but thank-you for this gracious visit. I will call you later today to arrange our next appointment."

As I drove away, with his arms full of cat, George waved to me.

• • • • • • • ● • • • • • • • •

The piercing jangle of the phone caused me to sit straight up in bed. I glanced over my snoring husband to the bedside clock. It was two in the morning. *Two.* I grabbed the beige receiver. "Hello?"

"Mrs. G., hello it's me. I hope I didn't wake you but I'm very, very upset. I haven't eaten today and I can't sleep. I don't know how this happened … he always seemed fine. But. But … Silver died today. Sometime late this afternoon. There I said it."

"George is that you?" I held the phone close. George was crying and nosily blowing his nose. "George, I am so sad to hear this, you cared very much for Silver."

"Yes," he said clearing his throat. "Silver was my favorite. When he didn't come down for supper, I went searching for him. Found him upstairs under the guest bed. I carefully pulled him out and he was very still. His wonderful purring was gone."

"Did you take him to the vet?"

"I called right away. But when I described Silver's condition the doctor only confirmed what I already knew—that Silver was dead. He recommended that I bring him in tomorrow at nine to make arrangements for either a usual burial or cremation. I just finished covering Silver and put him in the cool garage." Sobs erupted and George became inaudible.

"George, I can't hear what you're saying. We need to meet. Plan to see me tomorrow. Please call when you're finished at the vet hospital. For the rest of the evening, I suggest you try to calm yourself. Why don't you sit in your favorite chair with a cup of that special tea you love?"

"Mrs. G. I can't sleep so that might be a good idea. I'll also play my classical music."

"Please take care. I am very concerned for you. See you in a little while."

· · · · · · · · · ● · · · · · · · ·

A few hours later found both of us in seat, neither of us had slept. In that session and others to come, George wrestled with death. Questions and more questions. Why did Silver have to die of a heart attack with no warning? Why did he feel so guilty—what did he miss? Why couldn't he go back in time? The burial issues were an assault on his heart. How could he just put Silver in the cold ground or worst yet, burn him into ashes? Yet the veterinarian had urged a response—today. George wanted to do the right thing for Silver. He decided he wanted something left of Silver, so he chose cremation.

Years have passed. George no longer has any cats. Instead he changed jobs and works as an assistant manager in a golf shop which he thoroughly enjoys. He has made new friends and enjoys playing a round of nine holes.

And as far as I know, George keeps several metal urns specially placed on the fireplace mantel, polished and lustrous.

## ESSENTIAL MATTERS
### *When You Least Expect*

On occasion I will pick up a compilation paperback—that is a book of lists. So I've decided to write a short list of my own, looking at unusual happenings in a very usual counseling office. It is especially interesting when ...

the soothing sound machine timer begins to beep like an ambulance.
the paintings in my office are getting all the attention.
the scheduled client changes from no shows to frequenting the office.
the last appointment left me a gift and it isn't Christmas.
the entire family of a client calls for an appointment—this one is great!
the new client is dressed to the nines prompting me to put on my winter coat.
the combo sub is repeating on me creating pungent aromas.
the decorative office candle is lit to mask such odors.
the sofa has secreted enough spare change to order a pizza.
the next client woke me from a short nap between appointments.
the jam from the peanut butter and jelly sandwich smeared my chin as the session began.
the sensor light clicks off and I can't see my client
the client I'm waiting for is actually scheduled for this time ... next week
the heat is blasting and I throw my head out the window.
the beloved office chair swivels off kilter, leans over and crashes to the floor ...
and that's all for now.

It's astonishing in this world how things don't turn out at all the way you expect them to.

                                                            Agatha Christie

# Chapter Thirteen

## The Zone

Here is an interesting case—off the worn path. Actually there is some self-disclosure, this one is one me.

Here it goes. When the door opens and a client enters the counseling domain readiness is essential. It is necessary to put aside personal cares and concerns and tune into the client's wavelength. Put on her sandals or his loafers and experience the blisters. This sounds easy but speaking for myself and other professionals, this isn't so.

Today on the way to the office a truck bullied me out of my lane which compounded the argument I had had with a neighbor. Now the vague tingling in my head upgraded to sledge hammering. Positive self talk was wrestling with fuming car woman as I turned the lock to the office door. Shortly there would be seated a most anxious client who required full attention.

Get with the program right now!

I sat in my favorite seat and embraced the relaxation and visualization exercise often encouraged for clients. Ten minutes later my client arrived and I was as ready as I was going to be.

The session unfolds as planned. That is what generally happens.

But on occasion our efforts can yield extraordinary results. This is about one of those times.

• • • • • • • • ● • • • • • • • •

A few years ago my hip began misbehaving. I would be walking when powerful aches would grab my attention. Without warning—I could be gardening or having lunch—shooting pain radiated through my upper thigh leaving me breathless. Visits to orthopedic specialists yielded some clarity; that I was fifty-something and gimping about with the hip of an eighty-year-old. And did I know why? I should say not. If anything I was hoping for their flash of brilliance. But they were all stumped. Collectively they recommended full hip replacement. I balked. Wasn't there something else? Physical therapy might bring some relief. Indeed two years of regular hands on manipulation helped. Yet there were days nothing eased the pain. The hazy fog of the inevitable circled. Surgery. They told me I would know when and it was coming.

Then came a morning I felt fine. It was a glorious spring day that urged planting geraniums and daises. With light melodies dancing in my head, I was anticipating today's session with Mary. She called me Mrs. G. but was insistent on using her first name. This was our third appointment and I had appreciated our verbal exchange immensely. This feisty forty-year-old woman was made of tough stock. Not a woman of means but she displayed strong character and a smile that could light Central Park. Hard work was her forte. She been a nanny, worked in a nursing home, cooked for a diner. Currently a bus driver, she was taking classes to become a physical therapist—a childhood dream.

She had the grandest heart, always ready to embrace and offer a good word. Most impressive was her witty sense of humor; gregarious and full of spontaneity. People would flock around her like children at a pizza party. Besides working and attending classes, she cared for relatives that lived above and below in their three floor apartment house. She was always running to and fro with some errand. These interruptions did not discourage her generous spirit, she was just like that. Thus far our sessions had been upbeat, as Mary detailed situations attempting to cut and paste her life. Ever flowing optimism was a continual flame.

But not today.

I knew something was awry with only a glance. Mary's usual decorum donning bold color and jazzy style was off. Her outfit was mismatched and her gaze was distant. Even her favorite sports cap hung oddly on head. Mary's overall carriage was awkward, her affect dull. Finding her usual seat, she plopped down. Her large hands trembled as she placed them awkwardly on her lap. Her sepia eyes were full of remorse and sadness. Today there were new fields to plow.

"Good morning Mary." I rose to shut the door making sure the white noise box had not tangled in the entrance. Suddenly a jolt crashed through my hip leaving me airy. For a long moment I stood immobilized, under attack from my own body. Lightheaded and confused, I put one foot in front of the other and sank stiffly into the desk chair. I peered cautiously over at Mary who seemed not to have noticed my dilemma. I was in melt down. Readjusting my position wasn't working. I could hear the ailing hip pounding in my ears. I looked over at Mary. A preferable choice would be to send her home.

"Mrs. G. it's not a good morning for me. You see, I'm very worn out. With all I am doing, my father is sick as well and I have to help him. He is a very stubborn man." Mary paused and righted her posturing, giving me full eye contact.

I wanted to reschedule this appointment but instead responded, "Mary, when you came in I knew that something wasn't right. With all your responsibilities you have an additional burden of helping your father." I swiped my forehead realizing I had opened Pandora's Box. What was I doing? I should be going home. I steadied my trembling hands.

"Yes. I have been going to his apartment which is a couple towns away. Not too far, but with traffic and when it gets late, ugh, I've been sleeping on the coach. This is no way to live!"

"You're very irritated. Mary, you're such a generous person. But this situation is putting you over the edge—with the change of routine, lack of sleep ..."

I'm not doing anything right. I'm having trouble studying and I'm making mistakes at work. Everything would be better if I could have my father live with me. I have plenty of room—it's a big three story house. But he is difficult, I know he won't come."

"You haven't asked him yet. You're assuming that he will decline."

"That's right. It's because—well, I haven't told you this. He isn't my real father. When my father died I had no one so my uncle brought me up. He was so kind to me. Bought me nice clothes and always fed me well. He even braided my hair. I would do anything for him which is why I'm staying at his place. The reason why I know he won't come to my house is because he doesn't get along with these relatives. They are family from my mother's side—remember I told you my mother had died in an accident—and they didn't help me when I was young, so he resents them. But they seem okay with him."

The pain in my hip was throbbing; if I so much as move ...

Mary's eyes met mine. So hopeful. Waiting for encouragement. Direction.

I nodded and shared.

She did the same.

Our thoughts enfolded as understanding flowed smooth as pure deep chocolate among the sparkling stars of the Milky Way. Time was limitless. We had stepped into a kind of alternate reality.

I was my mind not my body. It was a mind full of clarity and dreamlike visions. The crashing hip no longer registered. Instead thoughts were connecting. Empathic. Enlightened. Full of sage intelligence.

Mary's emotions were as fluid as from a painters brush—swirling brilliant color creating cosmic delight.

I etched in delicate lines. She blended in vivid hues.
There were spilled tears.
Quivering lips and open hands.
Soulful sighs.
A serendipitous exchange resplendent with wisdom.
We had bonded together in an awesome moment.
Not soon to be duplicated. If ever.

• • • • • • • • ● • • • • • • • • • •

I looked over at the leather chair. Mary's smile was radiant. Her hands were gesturing wildly with expression. Mary was back, renewed and fresh—full of hope. Emotions and upset had played out and resolve found. There was much to be done. Armed with new direction Mary couldn't wait to get started. First on her docket was to take her father to supper and have a heart-to-heart talk. Tell him how much she cared and how much she wanted the best for him.

Mary suddenly stood, her eyes meeting mine. Comforted. Relieved. She grabbed my shoulder and gave me a warm hug. Our visit had gone over but neither of us cared. We knew something special had happened.

I sat relishing the afterglow. The sweetness of the session hung in the air. Something powerful had occurred. We both had fully engaged ourselves; Mary embracing her pain and me, casting it off. We had opened a door to another time, another place—an alternate zone.

• • • • • • • • ● • • • • • • • • • •

Several years have gone by. But this session imprints on my memory in a remarkable way. Firstly, this kind of a tunnel experience has not happened again.

However the connection with Mary remained. Continuing sessions were productive so that in a few weeks Mary was on her feet and marching. I was delighted to see this determined woman renew her vigor and vitality. From brief letters I found that Mary had successfully accommodated her father and relatives and her life-long vocation as a physical therapist. So many good things; perhaps even romance would kindle for her.

I hoped the best for Mary. As far as I know she is enjoying life.

Shortly after that legendary visit, my hip was successfully replaced. I walk just fine and even work out at a nearby gym. Yet I have often mused on that extraordinary session. How did it happen? Was it the intensity of pain we both were experiencing? Why then? Would it happen again?

Most of the time I press forward; offering a listening ear to a given client. I stay focused, genuine in my desire to journey with them. Discovering briar-filled pathways, stepping in muddy puddles and slipping on wet stones certainly can make this journey interesting.

But once in a while I wonder if the zone will reopen.

# ESSENTIAL MATTERS
## Choices

I was stuck in the produce section. I had spent way too long in the apple aisle. Should I buy the tart green grannies and make a pie or some juicy ones for snacking? I held apple after apple up to the light to check for freshness, for a blemish of any sort. Most enticing were the bold colors and the mouth watering aromas. I waved a plastic bag as I hovered over the luscious assortment.

Decisions. There are so many possibilities to pick from. In a single day there are probably hundreds of choices made. Consider the first course of decision-making, the ordinary in the everyday tasks. The early morning begins with figuring what to eat for breakfast, what soap to use, what tasks have to be done and if there is enough gas in the tank. Some call these chores daily living skills and there are common to all of us. These life fundamentals are vital to our lives.

The second course of personal choice lassoes the big decisions that shape our views, our actions, our very selves. This list considers education/career training, employment, marriage, children and housing. Once acquired there is the seemingly endless management of responsibilities as days flow into one another. As the years add up, the third course reflects on those past choices and hopefully savors a life well-lived.

For right now my focus is on apples. I think I will buy enough for healthy snacking and some for a luscious baked pie. Just for fun I'll go back to get some vanilla ice-cream and dollop every piece.

I can't wait.

Love is patient and kind; love is not jealous or boastful; it is not arrogant or rude.

Love does not insist on it won way; it is not irritable or resentful; it does not rejoice at wrong bit rejoices in the right. Love bears all things, believes all things, hopes all things, endures all things.

1Corinthians 13:4-7, RSV

# Chapter Fourteen

## A Chance Encounter

Briskly walking, I hurried to the entrance of the neighborhood hotel that was hosting a professional seminar. I wanted decent seating, hopefully somewhere in the middle where I could both hear and see. And be somewhat incognito. A lovely petite woman followed me in boldly greeting me. Her broad smile was most welcoming and kind. Did I know her? She seemed familiar, but we had not met. Until now. We exchanged lively small talk exchanging reasons for attendance. She disclosed her nursing background and I relayed that I was a counselor. We might have sat together except once inside we were set adrift among the huge wave of participants. The morning key note speaker had begun.

During break times I scanned the plethora of tables hoping to locate my new acquaintance. Her expertly styled gray hair and deep mahogany skin made her a stand out. But she was nowhere to be seen. Then she found me. Before the afternoon session, there she was gushing with excitement and questions. It wasn't about the seminar. It was about me. She quickly detailed how she had been considering seeing a counselor and meeting me had stirred her interest. Would we be able to meet sometime?

For a slight moment I gazed over her head. I had not seen this coming. This situation hadn't happened before ... I was taken off guard. I felt a bit flustered and very much flattered. My eyes met hers,

"Of course I would be honored to meet with you." Digging into my purse I located a business card, handed it to her and continued, "My number is to the left, call me soon to schedule an appointment."

With a gleaming smile she nodded and agreed she would.

• • • • • • • ● • • • • • • •

Two weeks later I sat at my desk and readied a preliminary application for this new client. Over the phone Mrs. A. Harrison had given a great deal of information, but I figured there was more. Gleaned were marital status, current employment, financial situation and that she wanted to talk about her husband. Glancing at the door I was expectant. So often in this business, especially if working with referrals, the phone consult is all you get. Whatever facts in hand form some semblance of that person in my head. Sometimes reasonably accurate and other times I am way off my mark. But not today. We had had a serendipitous meeting. I was looking forward to being of good service.

Suddenly the door swung open and there she was.

"I'm so glad to be here," exclaimed Mrs. Harrison, grabbing my hand, warmly shaking it. "You know I went home really thinking about how we met … that maybe I was jumping too quickly into something. I even went online and looked up your credentials. The more I read the more I knew seeing you would be the right thing. So here I am!"

"I'm pleased as well. Our introduction was unusual and special. I'm looking forward to our session," I said as I handed her the intake packet and pen.

The office went quiet. Mrs. Harrison seriously focused on the paperwork.

I focused on her. Like our initial encounter, she was dressed on point, you would say, with fashion and design that accented her elegant form. Her wispy gray hair so complemented her high ebony cheekbones that I wanted to frequent her hairdresser. The maturity of this woman was shining through the accomplishment of her years.

I glanced at the completed paperwork as I offered comfortable seating. Also were indicated the locations of the waiting area and the bathroom. "Mrs. Harrison you mentioned there were many concerns. Perhaps there was one in particular even as you drove here. Yet when we met at the seminar I sensed there was a current issue you wanted you discuss."

Mrs. Harrison smiled and nodded. "Yes, you're right because on the way here I was thinking about my father and my upbringing down South. But that day I wanted to talk about my husband. She paused, gazing out the picture window.

"Hmm," I said thumbing through the packet. "You've written that your first husband died and that you remarried."

"Yes. After my first husband died suddenly of a heart attack, I was very depressed. I worked a lot. Things got better when I met Frank. He is a wonderful man, very gracious and thoughtful. We have many things in common like going to the movies and playing cards, but he also has his own interests which I respect."

Mrs. Harrison laughed. "For example, I can't stand golf. On weekends he glues himself to the television watching every tournament and he reads every golf magazine he can find. Frank used to play a great round of golf … but now, that's why I wanted to see you. Frank has been quite sick." Mrs. Harrison sniffed and wiped tears from the edges of her sorrow filled eyes.

"You love Frank and you're worried about his health. Your heart is heavy having to care for a sick husband."

"I am very worried. Frank has a serious cancer. I've been trying to help him every way I can. Being a nurse, I have provided additional help for him at home. We have had countless radiation treatments and office reviews. But recently there has been a new development that found my husband in remission, that is many of the symptoms are less severe and some I don't notice anymore," Mrs. Harrison said soberly as she cleared her throat and moistened her lips.

"Something about this diagnosis upsets you. This should be a time for celebration but you're wary. Perhaps you think that this news is too good to be true."

She nodded. "Even though the doctors are positive, I don't feel this way. You're right it sounds too good ... Frank could still die. Yet he supposedly is fine—at least for now—and I need to enjoy him and stop treating him with special gloves."

"But you are finding this extremely hard to do."

"I guess all my experience in nursing has caused me to be guarded. With cancer or with any illness there are so many outcomes."

"Mrs. Harrison, you're facing your husband's illness with realism, knowing what could possibly happen. Frank's improvement had not settled you; instead you are worried and scared."

"I keep thinking that this remission is temporary and that he will suddenly get worse. My stomach is in knots thinking that they or I missed something—that Frank is sicker that we think."

You're feeling a huge weight of responsibility. You love you husband and want to do everything you can for him. You're concerned that maybe there's more you can do and you're very anxious."

"Yes. I want to enjoy my husband but I can't relax because I keep thinking the worst." Mrs. Harrison dabbed her moist eyes that suddenly had grown deep circles underneath them.

"You have taken on so many roles. Wife. Nurse. Daily care taker. All this has tired you so that you don't feel like yourself."

"I know I am overtired since I don't rest that good. Often Frank wakes and wanders about until he falls asleep in his recliner. After that, I can't get back to sleep. During the day naps are hard to come by. Taking care of him all the time I feel like I am walking about in a daze."

"Yet you're here ... is your husband is home taking care of himself? Has something changed?"

"As a matter of fact it has. A couple of weeks ago I was able to connect with a respite service—professional care-workers who provide service at home to give the family a break. Insurance pays a small portion of this expense; the rest comes from my pocketbook. But it's worth it because I'm able to leave the house. Right now a wonderful young man is visiting my husband. That is how I attended that seminar and was able to come here."

"Finding respite assistance has been a positive step; your husband has someone to help with daily activities and listen to his …"

"And I can go out to the store or visit friends. I need time to myself … it often feels like we're stuck together."

"Mrs. Harrison, this gives you space to refresh so that you can continue in your care giving duties."

"You're right. I'm working on a better attitude. I'm especially trying to understand Frank's relentless concern about our finances and family decisions." She chuckled and continued. "His constant meal planning and food shopping can make me crazy. But at least he has his appetite back."

The session went on a little longer—initial appointments tend to be this way—as Mrs. Harrison further detailed her situation. Since she wanted to work together with him in counseling, we decided to try both. Appointments were scheduled alternating a couples' session with those weeks Mrs. Harrison came alone. Her homework that week—to invite her husband to the next visit.

· · · · · · · · ● · · · · · · · · · ·

The following week I heard a flutter of happy commotion down the hall. In bounded Mr. and Mrs. Harrison, filling up my cozy office. They were two singing birds on a branch, chattering like they were at a party instead of a counseling office. The atmosphere had become festive and I almost wondered why they were here. Almost. Then the bickering began; where was the best place to put their coats and what were the choice seats. Being on the rotund side,

Mr. Harrison scrutinized every option before sitting on the coach allowing just enough room for his wife to squeeze in. There they sat with calm smiles and hands touching. Now here's a couple that, while they may have their disputes, clearly evidence a fondness for each other.

Our bi-monthly meetings were like sipping a hearty red wine, full and robust. We covered much ground. Honestly they voiced their upsets. Mr. Harrison, dapper in his plaid vest and tie, displayed proper manners and while annoyed with his wife's constant hovering, he took care not to offend her. Mrs. Harrison responded in kind; while extended with health care efforts and often impatient with her husband's constant focus on finances and food, she attended to him with a loving heart. They both laughed easily—finding humor in their humanness. What they could change, they set their minds to, and what could not, they accepted. Ample forgiveness was shown. Tender expressions were often seen; a hug, a kiss or even holding hands. They were compliant and ready to embrace the better portion of life. I was delighted to assist this couple—they were most welcome in my office.

As clients improve, sessions are spread further apart until one day it is time to launch. Such was the way with this kindly couple. With generous handshakes Mr. and Mrs. Harrison were send forth, acknowledging their success; offering an open door policy if they wished to return. I smiled and entertained hopes of seeing other couples that were so malleable and a joy to counsel.

• • • • • • • ● • • • • • • •

Then came the phone call. Mrs. Harrison's voice was soft and a bit raspy. A sense of foreboding clenched my chest. I sensed what she was about to tell me. "Mrs. Harrison, you don't sound like yourself today, like you may be starting a cold or …"

"Mrs. G., Frank died. Late last night."

I was stunned. My mouth went dry, words stuck in my throat.

After the moment of numbness a deep sigh rushed from my lips. But I heard myself respond with trifling words, "I am sad to hear this."

Not dissuaded by my humble reply, Mrs. Harrison launched into a detailed account and through ample tears told me what happened. After they had left my office things went well for awhile until Frank got sick again. Her husband spent a few weeks in the hospital and then was discharged. "My Frankie seemed alright until last night when I rushed him back to the hospital. And then he was gone ... it all happened so fast."

An appointment was scheduled for after the funeral—an event I attended. These were untried waters for me since I had not lost a client, and one involved in marital counseling, through death. I was experiencing loss as well. When Mrs. Harrison again frequented my office, I was looking for her husband to trail in and kindly help her remove her coat. Though a difficult time—our counseling relationship experienced a bonding that was heartfelt and productive. There was a shared mutuality.

Evidenced were the grief responses of depression and guilt. Over the weeks this was an intense concern; that she, Frank's wife, care taker and companion could have done more. She could have saved him. Such recrimination made it difficult to move forward and Mrs. Harrison spent much alone time at home surrounded by her life as it once was.

Depression hung heavy on her shoulders for weeks. Sadness clung to her like a dingy old cape. And that eager smile, full of life's goodness was a tight frown.

One day everything changed.

Mrs. Harrison came into the office filled with vibrant energy. Her first words were, "I have spent the past two weeks cleaning out my husband's closet. I donated to the used clothing store and gave stuff to the neighbors. Friends invited me to lunch and I also went on a day trip where Frank had often taken me." The story went on. Calls came in from family in her home town down South. Invited to return to her roots, she initially balked, but unexpectedly, a couple from church offered to buy her house. After that, a male friend from her hometown, having heard about her desire for part-time nursing work, offered a position. Mrs. Harrison, her eyes sparkling and cheeks aglow said, "Everything is happening so fast ... yet I think I just might say yes to all these offers."

Over several weeks Mrs. Harrison pondered and discerned. She wanted to honor her husband's memory. But she also wanted to be happy again. Was it possible to do both? Wouldn't Frank have wanted her to go forward and find a new way? Volleying these concerns she came to believe her husband would have wanted the best for her. In her heart, she decided to take Frank to the, "next chapter," of life.

With determination, Mrs. Harrison sold the house, and relocated to her home town. She accepted a part-time nursing position and purchased a spacious condominium. In one of her notes, she mentioned joining an art class—something she had always wanted to do—and was enjoying watercolors and fellow students.

Lately, I have not heard from this lovely woman, but I suspect it is because she has found satisfaction in that next chapter and is enjoying her new home sweet home.

# ESSENTIAL MATTERS
## *Noticing Every Face*

All of life matters. Life is important from the expected little one formed in secret to the testy adolescent in middle school to the gentleman taking deliberate steps with his cane. Of course, life matters to all of us in between.

Every person, in whatever stage of development is significant. Each face holds a story of its own—of joy and pain, accomplishment and struggle. Challenges enlighten and reap maturity as each individual moves their piece on that game board called life.

It is a privilege to wake every morning. We are given a gift to begin a new day embracing all the challenges whether thriving or difficult. There are the high fences to clear and the low to tunnel under. All of us are included. We recognize and honor each other—how old we are, where we live and what we do.

I notice you and you see me. We are everywhere. On the street corners, shopping at the super market, sitting in the city park. We are all travelers trying to find our way. Sometimes along that dusty road we can go past noticing to reaching out.

And simply say "hello."

Most people live and die with their music still unplayed. They never dare to try.

Mary Kay Ash

# Chapter Fifteen

## Jeannette Anne

Now I will return to that fresh faced youth attempting to take on the role of a professional worker—me. This story details my brand new position in a handicapped facility. In my twenties, I was hired as a rehabilitation counselor. I would be assisting at two sites; their renovated office complex and the alternate site, a fully operative factory that had leased a portion for rehabilitation use.

It was at this workshop that I met Jeannette Anne. She had worked there for sometime completing subcontracted piecework. A mini-van transported her every morning and given staff would assist at the door and escort this middle-aged woman to her seat.

Work would then begin.

• • • • • • • • • • ● • • • • • • • • • • •

It was my first day. And I was lost. I had been told that access to the agency's rented space was through a right hand doorway of the factory. But no one had told me what to expect upon entering. Mechanical shrills and whining screeched my brain accompanied by constant pounding and pounding and pounding. Behind the cacophony, I saw the workers' hands as well heads which were wearing protective gear. I wanted to block my ears but instead shielded my eyes. Everyone wore a gray apron that covered their dress down garb. Protective eyeglasses were in place and white masks covered mouths. The bitter stench of hot metal irritated sensitive nostrils and burned my throat. As soldering irons waved, red hot flares singed my perfectly combed hair. A dust cloud enveloped me causing directional confusion. Stern glances were cast, but I resisted the urge to run. Instead I placed hands at my side, walking with my head high and shoulders square—although hoping that no one would see my twitching eyes. I wanted this exuded confidence to catch up with my jittering insides.

Upon locating the familiar faces that hired me, I smiled and greeted them.

"Miss B. (maiden name), you took the long way in which can be quite dangerous," said Mr. Ford, a tall lanky gentleman man who would become my supervisor. He then shook my hand. "Good to meet you. Let me show you around." He spoke in a in a serious monotone but then flashed a huge smile at me.

"Staff offices are behind the cubicle windows. Over there," he pointed to his right, "is where the piecework is kept and once done is packed and trucked out the door you came in. The workers, we call them clients, are seated at the work tables but any needing special arrangements are placed to the left side. The client lunch room is behind us and the staff kitchen and bathrooms are over there." He then pointed to a freshly painted blue door and said, "And this is the counseling room." Nodding, I stepped in and noted the plain desk and functional folding chairs.

Mr. Ford continued. "You probably won't use this place much since the clients don't like it." Noticing my surprise he added, "When someone is ready to talk it just happens." I wanted to ask him about the benefits of confidential exchange offered in privacy when he pointed to a woman across the room.

"There's your first assignment … Jeannette Anne. She appears to be having a bit of trouble today. See if you can get her seated which would be over there in the left line of tables, end chair."

I nodded and left the meager office. Other workers were bustling around Jeannette Anne—hanging jackets, leaving lunch boxes and seating themselves at long tables amply supplied with piece work. But this woman walked cautiously, looking down at each step as if a deep gorge would open and swallow her up. Her arms wrapped her midsection in a tight hug. She didn't seem to notice anyone else and for the most part the other clients avoided her—until one of the workers accidentally pushed her off kilter. Regaining balance, she waved her hands in attempt to rid herself of him. Irritated, she rubbed her forehead and proceeded to her work area.

Jeannette Anne dressed much nicer than the others in her fresh slacks, collared shirt and gray cardigan—even better than me. When I reached the assigned work area, I noticed her short hair was a bit odd, uneven and jagged with a bare spot here and there. Her slim physique suggested youthfulness but her face was ashen and creased with worry lines. Noticing me, she flashed a disgusted smirk. I wondered how to greet this surly temperament. A polished approach would impress my new boss and co-workers—but what would that be? I took a deep breath and held out my hand. "Hello I'm Miss B ..." Jeannette Anne turned her head and stared with suspicion. She walked abruptly to the other side of the room and paced army style on a thick runner—a rug that appeared to have been placed especially for her. She spoke angrily to herself.

"Hello." I stood a reasonable distance and watched this woman walk back and forth.

"Who are you?" Jeannette Anne cast a wary glance in my direction.

"I'm Miss B. I'm a new staff worker here. And you are ..."

"They call me Jeannette Anne." She forced a smile. "I need to get to work right now." She appeared flushed and loosened her collar. She walked quickly to her assigned work area and sat in the end seat.

Done. I had followed the supervisor's directive and was relieved that was over. I headed over to the office and as I passed Mr. Ford he chuckled and muttered, "We'll see what happens tomorrow."

• • • • • • • • • • • • • • • • • •

The next morning there was so much to get used to; it was a new job after all. I glanced over at Jeannette Anne. She sat and focused on her assigned work. The behavior I had witnessed the day before was like it never happened. I met many other workers that day—interesting men and women who were physically and mentally challenged, some were blind, others deaf, several maneuvered with canes, others were wheelchair bound. All had their stories, but for me Jeannette Anne's was most engrossing. She had my attention. The desire to intervene and offer support was overwhelming. But getting a well-rounded picture was somewhat elusive. The official file, which was secured in the main office, was very lean. She had been referred to this agency some six months ago and was still becoming known. What was detailed regarding her story was remarkable and sad. It turned out that Jeannette Anne had lived a "closeted life." She had been spent many years living solely with her mother since her father had died when she was young. When her mother became gravely ill, neighbors called for medical assistance. The medics arrived and found Jeannette Anne in a corner bedroom of the bungalow styled house. It was a small, dark room she had not left in many years—except to use the bathroom. Her mother had provided the simple necessities of living but had not involved her in many outside activities. Possibly the mother believed such arrangements were acceptable due to limited understanding of her daughter's condition. Perhaps there was a sense of awkwardness and shame. Since the mother had recently died, realizing a full accounting of these circumstances would forever be a mystery.

There was additional information but it was scant; Jeannette Anne had attended lower elementary grades and was suddenly removed. Since her mother passed, Jeannette Anne now lived with relatives but she withdrew herself from them. Medical history was lacking until just recently. The latest evaluation declared the classification—agoraphobia; fear of places or situations where escape is difficult—combined with panic attacks. These terms presented an accurate picture of Jeannette Anne. Indeed this woman displayed anxiety with her surroundings, encountering sudden moments of fear and upset. One entry described that depression would cloud her face like a dark mist and she would tremble, complaining of chest pain and abdominal discomfort. I had already witnessed these symptoms.

I had to help Jeannette Anne. I commissioned myself—with the permission and backing from the rehabilitation team—to utilize interesting methods to assist her. You see, this woman was full of contradictions and turmoil. While she could attend to her work she was a solitary person, wishing to be left alone. Contact with fellow workers provoked and distracted her. Jeannette Anne would then remove herself. Even coming to work was a prime challenge as her family coaxed her from the house into the agency van. Upon arrival similar aid from staff was needed.

It was time to develop a plan. The initial item involved a team effort that supported a fresh vision for Jeannette Anne. Next I worked on making light conversation with this client so as to build familiarity and trust. Taking copious notes, I observed her daily behaviors including given environmental conditions and changes. One morning—a particularly good day for this woman—I invited her to the counseling office.

"Jeanette Anne, I wanted to tell you that you're an excellent worker, completing your piece work acceptably and on time."

"Don't call me that! I hate that name. Call me Jean."

Her alarming outburst launched my insides but gently I said, "Jean is a fine name. From now on I will call you Jean and ask the staff to do so. Perhaps you would consider ...'

"Stop talking!" Jean abruptly stood and left the office and walked to the other side of the workshop and looked out the window.

I trailed a reasonable distance after her. I waited for her to calm down.

"It's certainly a lovely view. Perhaps sometime we can sit outside on the picnic bench." I hesitated, expecting an angry reply.

"That would be fine, Miss B. I would like very much to sit on the picnic bench at that building over there. I've never actually seen this bench but I hear people around me talking about it." Jean pointed to our office complex barely visible, about a block away.

I could hardly sleep that evening. My brain was sketching possibilities, making plans to move forward. I realized the counseling room was out and action was in. Exposing Jean beyond the walls may alleviate some of her fears and emotional turmoil. Tackling these afflictions, Jean could possibly take command of her world. I tossed and turned—my primary concern was that she might change her mind.

Amazingly Jean stayed the course. Each day we headed out I would secure her arm gently around mine. Sometimes I would gently coax. Other times I would remain quiet. The warm days of spring flowed into the months of fall. Our steps were sure but oh, painfully slow. Jean fatigued quickly. Commenting she was losing control we often returned to the factory. She would sweat, tremble and clench her stomach. Each step took decisive effort—it was grueling work but we moved in tandem like a well ordered walking machine. Patience was a key virtue, sharpened and honed as we both focused towards the goal.

Today my stomach clenched with excitement. This could be the day! Last week Jean was within a few feet of the picnic bench. Then the rains came and our walking tour was put on hold. But this morning the sun was aglow and beckoning. Optimistic this time, I packed a tasty lunch including Jean's favorites; corn ships, ham sandwiches and cupcakes.

Our walk felt electric. Jean seemed different. Before me was a woman whose gait had left hesitancy and taken on self-assurance.

She held her head confident, a sparkle lit her blue eyes, and yes, a wisp of a smile lightened her face. She chose not to take my hand but instead let her arms move freely in step. Jean had changed. Even if something happened and we didn't make it to that bench, I realized Jean had really succeeded. She became a conqueror.

I was proud of her.

· · · · · · · ● · · · · · · · · ·

Anyone coming by that weathered picnic table would have seen two women chomping on ham sandwiches and corn chips. However there was a grand celebration going on. Change has embraced us both and the moment felt surreal. The pomp and circumstance was not witnessed through sending balloons aloft or releasing doves. Instead there was a quiet joy. But I believe both our hearts were dancing a jig.

## ESSENTIAL MATTERS
*Relishing Those Moments*

The last client of the day had left. The spicy perfume she always wears remained a flowing mist in my office. A pile of paperwork was begging for fresh ink, but I chose to ignore it. It's the end of the week and I was in a melancholy mood.

I wanted to sit and reflect. So many upsets, so many needs were visited this week. Every client mired deep in the complexities of life. I had done my best to be present to them all. The objective counselor in me had witnessed them from afar but the subjective, truly impassioned side showered great warmth and concern. These clients have become part of me in a mindful embrace. They are no longer distant, but fully real and connected.

These individuals have journeyed diligently realizing progress and growth. I was learning from them as well—a wonderful sense of reciprocity. I envisioned each story as a lovely pie representing their life. Sometimes it was shared in generous portions, other times sparse pieces were cut as trust was fortified. Tasting their slice, I reviewed life circumstances with them. Welcomed into their reality, I tasted the sweet, sour, the bitter and unsavory in their lives. I sought to understand and offer new direction. The essence of tangy strawberry rhubarb lingers on my tongue. I was present to their distress for in many ways I have been there. I hope, even if only in part, to bring resourceful direction to many others; unveiling a new tomorrow. As time goes by and the exacting details may fade, these memorable encounters will stay with me.

You never know when sipping relaxing tea; you should have chosen morning espresso.

Johnna Anne Gurr

# Chapter Sixteen

## A Night Visitor

Checking the door knob with a quick jiggle, I was satisfied the office was secure. While I was heading home and soon would be wearing the family hat, my professional persona remains. That attainment to positive character and genuine benevolence continues its bloom. Other domains may challenge these principles including the most common circumstances in our days. A long line at the gas station. Reaching for the check book in the grocery store and realizing you left it on the kitchen table. Gulping down the details from the orthodontist that treatment for your youngest will tally thousands of dollars. These are possibilities that could unravel the best of intentions, undo the finest of integrity—or strengthen them.

The following vignette is somewhat out of the ordinary. I was prompted to fully engage my counseling side even though the day had ebbed and it was time to enjoy soft classical arrangements. The kitchen table had become the office. In this scenario my peaceful countenance was seriously compromised.

I was scared to death.

· · · · · · · ● · · · · · · ·

I was seated on my favorite coach, enjoying the warmth of several punched up pillows. A pile of books lay strewn about; one in particular was propped on my lap. Sipping a cup of honey herb tea, I leaned into the narrative to clarify a point.

A loud rap shook the carriage of the oak door. The outer storm door creaked as the late night caller demanded entry.

"Who is it?" I wondered who it could be at this hour and why they were so impatient.

The brass knocker slammed rigorously.

"Who is it?"

Someone was pounding the door! Someone was trying to break in! Icicles tingled my scalp.

Fight or flight.

It was decision time. My husband was away on a business trip and all four children were tucked into their covers dreaming of sugar plums. At least I hoped so. Should I grab a baseball bat or call 911?

But curiosity got the better of me as I stood on tiptoe and peered into the peephole. It was Joanie, a kindly friend from two blocks over. Now what would bring this woman out on such a chilly night?

I threw open the door.

"Joanie!"

The unkempt middle-aged woman brushed by me. Not apologizing for her brazenness she dashed into the welcoming warmth of the kitchen. I followed in the hulk like shadow of my friend.

"Joanie what is wrong? I've never seen you like this. Why you're sweating like crazy!" I ushered the hefty woman in blue jeans to a kitchen chair. Her pale skin appeared ghostlike in the shadow of the Tiffany lamp and her hands fidgeted with a tissue. Her tear-shaped gray eyes were clouded and confused, seeking my comfort. Instead I handed her the plate of this evening's baked chocolate chip cookies.

"Thank-you," she said as she crunched into the confection. "I've been through so much these past few days. I can't believe it, I just can't believe it," she said swiping the crumbs from her cheek.

"What can't you believe?"

"Oh, it's a long story and a very bad one."

"I want to hear your long story." I beckoned her to go on as I folded my hands on the table.

Joanie took in a deep breath. She twirled a strand of long salt and pepper hair. Then she rearranged her girth in the overused Captains' chair.

"Well it went like this. My chest had been hurting. I couldn't breathe right. I called for help. Some people came in a big truck and took me to the hospital. But it was not a hospital—I can't believe where they took me," she said as she waved her hands about like a zealous orchestra conductor.

"Where did they take you?"

"It was a terrible place … they were so mean to me. I think they called the place … I really don't remember."

"What happened there?"

"They tried to kill me! Look at this!" Joanie pulled up her soiled red plaid sleeve.

I gasped. The woman's plumb arm was blotched and bruised showing varying colorations of violet and black. "What happened to you?"

"Those awful people did this! They tied ropes to my hands and feet, then pushed me down on the bed. Then they …"

"Joanie, you were restrained?" I knew something had gone very wrong. Such severe agitation would have landed her in the psychiatric unit. Perhaps this was not a heart condition at all.

"Yes, these people were horrible. This one woman—I think she was a nurse—had a needle. She placed it in one hand and flicked it with the other and then pulled up my sleeve. She wanted to kill me!"

"Joanie, you believe this woman was trying to harm you?'

"Honey, haven't you heard what I've been saying? What happened was very bad, that nurse was out to get me!"

"Maybe they used restraint because you were so upset." I had to admit this story was into edging into a medical drama.

"Help me! Have you lost your mind?" Joanie's cheeks were flushed and her nose flared like a wild mare. "I had to help myself! I jerked so hard that my right foot came free. Then I kicked that crazy woman right in the face!"

"You kicked the nurse?"

"Yeah, the one with the needle and she really flew. She swore at me and stuck her ugly big nose into my face! And I spit into hers!" Joanie snickered as she wiped sweat from her neck.

"Joanie you feared for your life. You were scared and you fought your way out. Then what happened?" I was trying to understand although I was having difficulty suspending disbelief. Was any part of this story real or was it a product of an overexcited imagination? Or perhaps my neighbor was delusional?

"Some other people dressed in green scrubs came in. Then, you know, that crazy nurse with the nose gets all sweet. She untied me saying something about a misunderstanding. One of the other guys helped me off the table and when they were all talking I left."

"So you didn't get the needle?"

"No, thank God."

"But you went in for a possible heart attack. Didn't anyone check you for that? Could it be you were having difficulty with anxiety?"

"You don't get it, do you? I almost get killed and you ask stupid questions!"

"Mom, can I have a drink of water?"

I startled and almost fell off my chair. What was this? The children should be snoring by now. Tucked in and safe. I looked down with horror at my ten-year old, who was pulling on my shirt and pointing at Joanie.

"Who is this? Don't come near me!" said Joanie.

A glimpse of metal flashed.

A gun.

Were my eyes focused right?

Joanie jumped to her feet with incredible agility that belied her beefy figure.

"Stay away from me! Not another step," she shouted as she waved the black and silver hand gun.

"Joanie, please calm down. Let me help you figure all this out," I said as I slowly stepped in front of my daughter, shielding her from harm. "Put the gun on the table so we can talk …"

"How can you help? You don't even believe me!" Joanie moved towards the back door.

"Joanie, I'm not sure what's going on, that's all. Please come sit and have another cookie." As she edged closer to the table, I gave my daughter a shove into the living room where her brothers and sister were eavesdropping and pointed to their bedrooms.

Joanie looked at me, then at the two remaining chocolate confections. For a long moment she watched the door. She circled the table with halting, uncertain movement like a lioness scouting her prey. Taking a deep breath she plopped into the chair and slammed the gun on the table.

She reached for a cookie and I for the Smith and Wesson.

Icy and smooth, it fit snug in the palm of my hand. Seemingly harmless metal but staring at the barrel, I knew its evil potential was only a trigger away. I rested the firearm under the cushion of the chair near me, careful not to disrupt it. 911. I had to call them. But the telephone was on the other side of the kitchen. Too risky. I needed to connect with Joanie and distract her.

"So Joanie, last week you were telling me that you purchased a guitar and that you signed up for lessons."

Joanie shot me a wary glance but then her eyes seemed to focus. "Yeah, I wanted a twelve string but it was very expensive and hard to play so I got a six string." She tilted her head playfully and smiled. I'm really looking forward to starting my first lesson next week. I love folk music and if I learn fast maybe I can play at church." Now relaxed, she bit happily into the last cookie.

"I'm happy to hear you want to play guitar. It's a wonderful instrument and since you enjoy music, you'll have fun.

*Paid in Chocolate*

"Joanie, Joanie, are you in there?" Shouts and raps were coming from the front door. These were familiar voices—Joanie's family. I grabbed the gun and rushed to the door. In hushed tones I quickly detailed the situation and handed them the firearm which was carefully placed in a pocketbook. I ushered Joanie's daughter and her husband into the kitchen where Joanie was lining up napkins and spoons. Following a brief family discussion, they whisked Joanie out the door.

The ticking of the mantel clock and the hum of the refrigerator were the only sounds heard.

It was like it had never happened.

• • • • • • • • • ● • • • • • • • • •

I was unable to meet with these relatives and fill in the many absent blanks. I could only conjecture—the situation didn't make much sense. What had happened to my friend—had she found a den fostering evil intentions? Or was she making this all up? She could have been really sick, physically or mentally and was taking medication that was causing hallucinations. And the gun, where did she come up with that? Joanie had been so angry; I had never seen that side before. It had been downright unnerving ... the waving of that gun—probably fully loaded—and my four kids watching. There could have been a very awful outcome. I had to shrug off the thought.

A few weeks later, a moving van emptied out Joanie's house. As I drove past, I gawked out the driver's window looking for my friend but there were only workers running about. I walked over to them and asked about the family. One of the men shrugged, he had no idea where they were. Body language said please go away, which I did but slowly so as to peek into the backyard. Absolutely nothing.

I would like to consider a fairy tale ending where Joanie is living in a chalet and the air is sweet. She has regained her health and mind. But this probably isn't so. Perhaps she is residing in some urban apartment with a firearm under each pillow. Most likely neither is right—it could be that Joanie had been speaking the truth and even as I write this, she is tied to a table as weird experimentation is done. No one hears her cries and the woman with the bumpy nose gives injection after injection. The brick facility covered with twisted ivy hides in the shadows. It is so remote that no superhero will hear her plea and fly her away. Joanie is doomed.

I don't think so.

But I still have a terrible hollow feeling in my stomach.

I watch the daily newspaper to see if any doughy faced, big nose lady is pictured caught in the act with a needle in her hand. There is a particular interest in special research projects happening down the street—maybe there is a sinister scheme that has been uncovered. Hunting hesitantly through the obituary page, I wonder if Joanie will show up there. I hope not. Yet some facts would alleviate worry. I could put this entire scenario behind me. But like many things in life, often there is no closure.

· · · · · · · · · ● · · · · · · ·

A year later the phone rang. I was outside on a ladder painting the garage so it took a moment. The caller was persistent. Breathless, I grabbed the receiver. It was Joanie. She was agitated and speaking so fast I could hardly keep up. What I did hear was that she had left family, relocated to another state and was in the process of being evicted. Panicked, she asked if I could help. Then the line went dead. Multiple attempts to reconnect didn't work.

Just great. Now my friend was in another urgent predicament. All I could do was pray for the best and wait for the next phone call.

Hopefully it will bring good news.

## ESSENTIAL MATTERS
*Putting The Left Pant Leg On First*

I have to admit it; I am a creature of habit. My husband was the one who suggested that I try putting my left pant leg on first. Initially I balked. After all what does my husband know about such things? Doesn't he know everyone puts on the right pant leg first? Hmm. When he wasn't looking I gave it a try. For starters this style of dressing was annoying and uncomfortable. I reinforced efforts by experimenting several days in a row. Amazingly one day I put on the left pant leg without thinking about it. It felt good! I figured this was a pattern with other behaviors. I switched my wrist watch and combed my hair with the other, less dominant hand. I was proud of myself and shared this success with my husband. He winked, saying he already knew.

I felt like Santa, having to laugh in spite of myself. I had put myself through a new routine to alter behavior. This was all about change. Initially I had been resistive to seeing things differently. But doing the same things over and over can become dull and boring—like having English muffins every morning for breakfast or driving the same route to work day after day. I realized there was something refreshing and satisfying about making even a small adjustment.

Consider doing something different. Change one thing. It can be a small thing. This self-help directive is currently touted in many a paperback. I have to agree with it. To alter a current behavior is a challenging feat. This means consciously making the effort to think of a new way—a creative thought. With a measure of personal conviction, this novel thinking will hopefully rise to the next level—the deliberate action. And why I say deliberate is because change, however small, will require constant attention and reminder; you will be on your own case! Until one day there is an aha! moment where the action just happens.

So today consider putting on the left pant leg before your right. You may like it.

If told something is impossible, find another hammer, more nails and a sturdier wall.

Johnna Anne Gurr

# Chapter Seventeen

## Stuck With His Keys

The first time I met Ms. Whitaker I thought she was a movie star. She had dropped by the office to make an appointment. "No, I can't stay," she said, her ebony hair flowing about her elegant form as she spoke. Simply wearing dark slacks and a white top, held the aura of importance, commanding attention. She moved with grace and refined etiquette. However seen in her sparkling smile was a false brilliance—her affect was a tad off. Something wasn't right. But of course she had initiated this appointment so there had to be a concern. When I had requested the reason for this session—as I generally ask all new clients—she left me her full name, address and current insurance but declined further details. She would do so when we met. My ears were ready.

- - - - - - - - ● - - - - - - - -

"Well Ms. Whitaker, usually new clients sit at the desk."

After a promising initial greeting, I handed Ms. Whitaker an intake packet to complete. Interestingly, she had chosen to negotiate the rocking chair and the clipboard. The young woman removed her cape coat and snuggled it around herself as she wrote. Looking up she said, "Yes, like you mentioned, counseling can be a good experience so here I am."

"You've made the right choice," I said smiling at the woman

dressed perfectly in designer jeans and matching boots. Salon waxed eyebrows arched just so as she completed the documents. Her make-up was smooth perfection although her lovely peach cheeks would be fine without any. From my desk, I quickly glanced to check her progress and offer assistance. Soon we would finalize with signatures and move on.

"Well, this paperwork looks to be in order," I said placing the packet aside, adjusting my seat in comfortable proximity to my client.

"Well," Ms. G.," began Ms. Whitaker, "I decided to call you because my life is a big mess right now. Let me explain. Recently I finished my degree in business management and instead of working for someone else, which I've already done, I want to open my own boutique. I've been planning this for years and have been waiting for the right time." She paused and eyed me expectantly.

"Ms. Whitaker, these are exciting plans. First I would like to congratulate you on your degree. You're a young woman determined to realize your own success plan. Yet I'm sensing hesitancy, there are obstacles in your way ... as you said your life is currently a mess."

"Yes, while I've become educated, I've made some stupid mistakes. When I was younger my mom pushed me into modeling and for awhile I did everything she asked. Even in my teen years, I went along with it. I loved wearing gorgeous clothes; but I didn't like the photo shoots and being stared at. What I really hated was that people looked at me like I was dumb. But I'm not!"

"Your childhood appears to have been bittersweet ... there were many ups and downs with modeling. Before me I see an intelligent woman who has completed her schooling and is preparing for a good future."

"Yes, I even graduated with honors. But like I said, my life is a disaster. While I wanted to please my mother—my father had left us years ago—I finally rebelled. Once I hit eighteen I quit modeling and took off with my boyfriend. My mother was furious. But I didn't care. I just wanted out. So we lived together in a roomy apartment which was alright until … until things got bad with him."

"You left home with a lot of tension between you and your mother. You were growing up. But your decision became troublesome. This boyfriend was a support for awhile until the relationship got rocky.

"I wanted so much to make things good. I have tried. I really have. You see, he has two sides—a loving, kind nature and a jealous, violent side." Ms. Whitaker rolled up her elegant blouse to reveal scars on her arm and wrist. "This happened because he thought I didn't go to the store but was cheating on him."

"Ms. Whitaker, this is abuse! This is not acceptable! Have you considered calling the police and pressing charges? Or finding another place to live?"

"Yes. I called the police once; they took a report and said I should leave. I stayed with a friend for a couple of days. Then my boyfriend said he didn't mean it. He said he loved me and wouldn't do it again. I went back. I loved him too, so I forgave him and even dropped the charges. But he didn't change. He kept beating me."

"You were smart to call for help. But your heart was soft and you're back with him. I'm concerned what the situation is like now. As a reminder, the papers you signed agreed to the *duty to warn*. It is my responsibility to protect you and secure help from any source possible, including contacting the authorities."

"I realize all this. But you don't have to worry. Some bad stuff went down awhile ago and he went to prison. That was two years ago and in that time I finished school, and kept up with his apartment.

"Ms. Whitaker, did I hear you right, that you are tending to the apartment that you both lived in together?"

"Yes, I promised that I would have it ready for his return. I visit him at the prison and we frequently write to each other. He always says he loves me.

"And you love him?"

"I'm not sure. That's why my life is so crazy. Part of me wants to have him back. I want some of those good times again … before he got so mean. Who knows maybe he's changed and become a better man? But mostly, I'm really scared. He won't like my idea of opening a dress shop and once he finds my savings, he will spend it all. And then he'll probably beat me."

"Ms. Whitaker, consider making the choice to leave, now! How much time do you have before he comes home?"

"That's a real problem. This is all kind of a sudden; he is coming out on parole the end of the month. Three weeks and four days to be exact."

"This gives you some time to relocate … although you are conflicted about leaving him. Perhaps he will come home a changed person and treat you with respect. Or he will pick up where he left off and abuse you."

"Mrs. G. you're right. I'm hoping for the best but I realize that it could be even worse than before. I understand you're under obligation to steer me away from harm; *that I should leave him*. Part of me knows that's the right thing to do but I made a promise to be here."

"Ms. Whitaker you made that promise with good intention, the intention being that you would help him so in return he would regard you with concern and decency. There is no evidence that he will comply even though he speaks kindly and …"

"But what about the parole? They're letting him come home early because he has shown good behavior. Doesn't that count for something?"

"In prison he was able to show good behavior with the hope of release. However there is no certainty that he has changed the way he handles a relationship. You may be putting yourself in harm's way."

"If you could only meet him, Mrs. G. He can be a wonderful man. He is generous, always buying me things and taking me out places." Ms. Whitaker paused and fingered the potted plant. "But then there is the dark side when he's depressed and gets really angry and blames me for everything. I have hopes and dreams that sometimes I think he could care less about."

"Dreams like finishing school and opening your own boutique?"

"Yes. Like I said before, these plans will irritate him and won't work. I should probably leave, after all he has hurt me, but I feel guilty not keeping my promise to be here."

Ms. Whitaker began to sob. Handing her tissues, I stood beside and gently consoled her.

• • • • • • • • ● • • • • • • • • •

In the remaining three sessions, viable solutions were firmly advised. While Ms. Whitaker spoke of guilt and personal honesty, she was not naïve to the fact she was risking personal safety. She realized her desire to have it all—a steady relationship, upscale housing, a career as a business woman. Such hopeful expectations met with a sense of foreboding. Moving forward meant fresh planning which had to begin with optimism. Ms. Whitaker finally made a decision to leave her boyfriend and relocate out of state. Temporarily she would stay with friends until she could establish herself. She planned to leave a brief departure note for her boyfriend with no forwarding address.

The last time I met with Ms. Whitaker she was confident and unwavering in direction. Dressed smartly in travelling clothes, her hair newly styled in an attractive page boy, she was ready to go. I wished her well with a tight handshake and off she went. I watched from the window as she jammed herself into a hatchback that was loaded with all her belongings. I waved goodbye.

Smiling she waved back. Ms. Whitaker went on her way to a brand new life.

## ESSENTIAL MATTERS
### *Just How Long*

Sometimes life is lived in the "in-between". This is the resigned place of uncertainty like the elevator that is stuck between floors. While so wanting to move up, it would be best to return to the main level and get out.

Many expressions of emotions can happen in this situation, you may be thinking of some right now. Personally I believe I would be yelling and screaming and hopping around. Instead of such an embarrassing outburst, I would rather approach this elevator conundrum with a bit of dignity and composure.

I would rather use patience.

There I've said it. Over the years I have been told be patient. I shudder, trying to shake this lesson off. My insides resist like a thirteen-year who desires to be dropped off at the mall to meet friends—now. All that wanting, all that anticipation put on hold. Stay where you are a little while longer. Just wait.

So much of life is lived in that in-between place where activity has slowed to the point of being interminable. A place so tiresome, I can't bear looking at the clock. Instead I negotiate, wake me up when this circumstance improves.

Patience requires a facelift on attitude. Embracing a peaceful, steadfast focus while enduring such detainment is the response I really want. Personal integrity can be gleaned from that in-between place if the right mind-set is embraced. Such long-suffering will eventually lead to the prize—of becoming a contented patient person.

Ugh.

I swiped the sweat off my forehead and took a deep breath. The elevator has finally begun to move.

Do what you can, with what you have, where you are.

Theodore Roosevelt

# Chapter Eighteen

## All Nerved Up

Today a man in his mid-forties, Mr. Fiddet, was reminding me of our initial counseling visits. He was seated awkwardly in the rocking chair and was moving with intense vigor. A tattered piece of material, called a worry rag, he twisted and twirled around his fingers. His polyester shirt and pants were dingy and his graying hair was in bad need of a comb. His sneaker clad feet danced a jittery tune all their own. Muttering about the terrors in the world around him, his voice swelled and ebbed. Personal self-esteem hovered on fumes. I attempted to secure personal eye contact with him but was not succeeding.

In earlier counseling sessions this man had limited focus, requiring additional help. Medication would possibly make the difference. Since I do not write these scripts, I referred him to a mental health prescriber and agreed to maintain current counseling. Mr. Fiddet initially declined but changed his mind, deciding to give medication a try. He responded quickly to this regime; with accompanied therapy and responsible personal application, ample progress was seen.

But today was different. This gentleman had serious business to reconcile and had slid into some of his previously witnessed behaviors. Our session opened awkwardly as this gentleman spoke his mind.

· · · · · · · ● · · · · · · ·

"Ms. G., I've decided that I can't take life anymore. There's too much going on!" He rubbed the palms of his hands on his cheeks. A flash of anger swept his face as Mr. Fiddet resumed weaving his worry rag thorough his fingers.

I had hoped to catch his eye but could not. "I'm concerned for you. We have discussed a great deal these past months and you've made good progress. Since we last met, you've encountered additional difficulties."

"Yes, yes. Sunday was the anniversary of my mother's death two years ago—remember we talked about her—and this sad memory reminded me of my wife's death. Why do so many awful things happen to me? I was even afraid to get out of bed and come here today. Because there's so much going on ... if my wife could die in a car accident, then what's to stop a bad man from running me over or shooting me?" He tilted his head and scratched a balding spot.

"You're right. I'm also saddened to remember this anniversary. There is much upset in the world today and terrible things could happen to us. But ..."

Mr. Fiddet snickered. "Yeah, I know what you're going to tell me. We've been over this stuff over and over. I tell you how I could get sick and die from the food I eat or that someone could break into my house and steal my stuff. A huge bomb could end the world or better yet, an asteroid could fall out of the sky and kill us all!" He paused and looked down at his feet.

"And what have we discussed?"

"That these things could happen but thinking about them all the time just makes me more and more scared. All this worry is stealing my life away ... I need to live my life."

"You have been trying to live your life," I said with an affirming nod. "When you first came to see me you were having trouble with your job, you couldn't eat right or sleep well at night. But you considered available choices and realized new directions, which you have successfully attempted. Now what you have here is a setback—reminders of losing your wife and mother are painful to you. You're feeling sad and lethargic which is causing you to backslide into some of your old behaviors."

"Yes, I'm very miserable. But wouldn't you be too? I get upset about all these bad things but doesn't everybody feel the same way? All these catastrophes give me headaches. I feel helpless." He shook his head back and forth.

"You're not alone. Most of us experience pain in life. Many people worry about the unsettled world picture … how these happenings influence their own lives. Myself included. The difference is a matter of choice; to succumb to these difficulties or to press forward."

Awareness flickered in Mr. Fiddet's deep brown eyes and his brows arched. "I understand what you're saying. I've done better. For one thing, my job isn't just a job anymore, it defines who I am. I used to think I was only a guy who cut lawns, but now I'm a man who loves to cultivate plants and see them bloom. I am working with the nurseries and becoming a master gardener. I really enjoy what I do."

"Yes, you're becoming more and more confident. You've been able to enlarge your vision and become skilled and self-assured. Having this sense of purpose can give satisfaction to life."

"Mrs. G., I agree. But I've been depressed these past few days. The changes I have made don't seem to matter. Even the meds I've been taking because of your recommendation aren't working. I think maybe I should stop taking the pills. Maybe even stop coming here."

"Everything at this time is such a struggle. Yet life happens with its up and downs. Overall you've done well and I believe that the medication has had its place in helping you stay balanced. As I said before, while I do not prescribe, I realize the importance of managed medication. This regime can help especially if you do your part. As for coming to the office, I believe overall wellness is a combination of counseling, medication and your best effort."

"So you think that I can still go forward even though I think I've fallen off the cliff? That what I need to do is continue the work I enjoy, take my meds and come here?"

"I definitely do. At least for now. As time goes on hopefully you will fear less and experience more. And perhaps, with your doctor's approval, you may lessen or even discontinue medication. Our visits could eventually spread out until one day you would be on your own. However it plays out is your decision."

• • • • • • • • ● • • • • • • • •

Mr. Fiddet experienced a tough couple of weeks but was able to get back on track. He continued with the counseling sessions and kept up responsibly with his meds—reviewing the current medication plan with his prescriber. When his impish smile returned and the worry rag was discarded, I knew he was on an uphill climb. Good things began to happen. Opportunity to become a business partner in a nearby nursery came knocking. He heeded suggestions to seek other interests and discovered bird watching. This gentleman purchased an avian journal and went on personal excursions waiting and watching. Finding a bird watching club, he happily joined. But the best was yet to come—he met a kindly middle-aged woman with whom he would sit and track birds.

Mr. Fiddet stretched out his appointments in the office. He continues to take a lesser amount of medication and under doctor's advisement may discontinue it altogether. Becoming part owner in a nursery business has allowed financial security allowing for dinners out and small trips. This gentleman has decided to take on life and while there may be days of upset for the most part, life is good.

And I do believe I hear the clang of wedding bells.

*Johnna Anne Gurr MS, LPC*

# ESSENTIAL MATTERS
## *On Trust*

When I was a student in college a friend invited me to a dorm party. I hesitated but then decided to go. The modestly size room squeezed in a crowd of students. There were acquaintances present, but many I didn't recognize. And wouldn't you know it … I had arrived just in time for the games. They were in the middle of something called the Trust Fall. Suddenly a group of gals and guys circled around and shouted at me to just fall backwards. "Don't worry we'll catch you!" "Come on," they said, "you can do it." They cajoled and pleaded.

I fell.

WOW! It was awesome. I couldn't stop laughing. Clearly I should not have put my life in their hands. After all I hardly knew any of them. For an instant I envisioned myself a pile of broken bones on the floor. But the next moment I leaned back and let myself go. I landed in strong, friendly arms that supported and gently laid me on my back. I had taken the risk and I was proud of it.

Somehow I had the nerve to trust. What is trust, really? For starters it can be a reliance on self to make good decisions. It is the similar ability to rely on others knowing that there is reciprocity in looking out for each other's best interests. We entrust ourselves in many ways; child to parent, student to teacher, friend to friend, spouse to spouse, worker to boss. There are many more. In particular there is the special trust relationship between client and counselor where steps are made in good faith to build a reasonable understanding. There is mutuality in genuine honesty. There is a confiding and yielding of personal details embracing all the upset and emotions. This relationship also ensures confidentiality which makes such disclosure private and discrete. Overall the desire is to advocate for improved life conditions with the aid of sound commitment from both parties.

Such trust takes time to develop. First comes the risk. Do I really want to do this? The odds are measured as possibilities are considered. Then comes the bold "yes" to the unknown. Trust can begin and grow … the free fall to something wonderful.

The source of continued aliveness was to find your passion and pursue it, with whole heart and single mind.

Gail Sheehy

# Chapter Nineteen

## Figuring The Family Way

I have often met with women embracing their childrearing years and are wondering, should I or shouldn't I? For some the maternal desire is intense; they want children right away! And in today's world those with given resources can even bypass marriage; choosing frozen embryos and surrogate nurturing. Others embracing customary unions or alternative relationships seek medical choices that promote opportunity for fertilization and hopefully a viable pregnancy. There are those couples that have chosen natural family planning and have successful pregnancies. Some expectant couples bare the sorrows of miscarriage, sometimes deciding to remain a family of two. Others examine adoption, the possibility of caring for children already born either newborns or those in their formative years. These are important choices especially noting the latter group of least desirable older children who so need this care. Have I covered it all? Well, I cannot forget those discouraged women who find their relationship in shambles and decide to part and be single once again.

Now those are the women and the couples who want children. But what about those who do not? I have found many a woman who would prefer to walk away from this entire messy affair. Pregnancy is disruptive, confusing, and expensive—a lifetime of costly responsibilities. So why exert the effort?

Instead some consider abortion. Not so messy or is it messier?

Working with women in a neighborhood pregnancy center, this option caused much consternation and twisting of heartstrings. Determining the direction of the family way embraces many emotions and outcomes. The abortion decision is huge—one that can be pressured by time factors and impact of bodily hormones as well as societal, family and faith-based viewpoints and customs. The question of a new life hangs in the balance.

I will introduce a twenty-something young woman, who I will name, Ms. Hedstrum, who for a number of reasons could not wrap her mind around a young one in arms. When Ms. Hedstrum initially called I could hardly understand what she was saying. Nearly breathless, her words were clipped and confused. Listening to her story, I prompted clarification and necessary details. Ms. Hedstrum had used a home pregnancy test—generally in office physician results are more accurate—and it was positive. She was certain she was pregnant. Ms. Hedstrum was bewildered and scared. She wanted to see me right away. Gathering as many details as possible, we scheduled an appointment. However before our visit, I strongly urged to see her personal doctor and confirm the finding; that she actually was pregnant.

• • • • • • • • ● • • • • • • • •

Collecting the finished paperwork I sat in my swivel office chair. Ms. Hedstrum chose the comfortable sofa. She positioned the pillows and smoothed the cotton jersey over her belly. "From reviewing your form, I understand that you're a patient of Dr. Jones, a local obstetrician. Were you able to see her this week?"

"Yes, yes. Dr. Jones is my mother's doctor. I made an appointment like you recommended. Dr. Jones told me what I already knew, I'm expecting. But I'm not sure I want to be."

"You're not feeling ready to have a child. Pregnancy can be a difficult time. It can also be one of life's most satisfying. Tell me, is this your first?"

"Yes. Although I think I came close a few times. I don't want to have a family like this ... this is not the way things are supposed to be." Ms. Hedstrum clasped her hands tightly.

"There are certain expectations you want that are not in place. This is very troubling to you."

"You're right. At my age I should be married, and totally moved out of my childhood home. I live with my mom and younger sister when I should be on my own."

"You're disappointed with your situation. You had hoped to be managing your own life."

"Well Ms. G., what I didn't write on those papers was that I left a couple of years ago. I lived with my boyfriend. I really thought he was a good guy but then he got weird. Friends of mine told me he was having a great time barhopping, meeting other women. I thought he was at work. That's what he told me and I believed him. I trusted him!"

"Ms. Hedstrum, you're so angry you could punch him! This was a heartbreaking time for you."

"It was awful. At first I made all kind of excuses for him. I guess I hoped he would see reason and change. Maybe marry me." Her golden eyes moistened.

"You were very distressed and irritated by your boyfriend's behaviors. Your hopes for marriage were unrealistic. You were unsure how to face him."

"Yeah. I decided to leave him. In the middle of the night I packed up and went home. He stalked me and I had to call the police. After a while, I heard he had found a good job and went to another state. Over the past year and a half or so things got a little better for me. I finished my certificate for office management and found a decent job in a company downtown. During that time I even met a new guy who is decent and asked me to live with him. I didn't want to. I want to be married. But he didn't. He took off and here I am here;

alone, the mother of his child. I can't believe all this ... he is so irresponsible."

"Ms. Hedstrum, you are pretty heated up with your current boyfriend. Finally you hoped he would be the one, instead he disappointed you. You must have been depressed but you still went on ... made some good choices like finishing school and getting a job."

"Yeah, now I'm pregnant. I wanted to be married and have a child. But have a child and be unmarried? Don't get me wrong, I love children, always have. I even helped my Mom with my sister. But how can I do this? Sometimes I think I should get an abortion. I'm only a few weeks along."

"You're very conflicted ... you're not sure what to do. This is a very perplexing situation. You mention abortion, which would mean ending the life of this child. But you have a heart for children and desire to marry and have a family. While the timing does not meet your expectation, having a child means a lot to you."

Ms. Hedstrum began to message her tummy. I couldn't do that to my child! Just get rid of it! Hey, this baby is already a he or she and not an "it" at all. I wouldn't be able to live with myself. And don't even mention adoption. I couldn't go through all this and then give up my baby to someone else. It's because I'm living home and all this is going to put a strain on my family. I have some savings, not much ... how did I ever get in this situation?"

"Ms. Hedstrum, you're frustrated. You wish you could change these mistakes. Yet you're human. Life is not perfect—it is important to do the best with what you have. You're looking at regret, what should have been and you're discouraged. Yes, it would have been convenient to marry and be sharing life with a caring spouse, yet you couldn't stay with someone you didn't trust. But you completed school and found employment. I commend you on what you have accomplished."

"What I have done? Boy, I really messed up." Ms. Hedstrum waved her hands awkwardly in front of her.

Realizing this woman had not fully heard me I reiterated. "Ms. Hedstrum you have wanted your own independence. This is a desired state especially for people your age. You tried by living with your first boyfriend and then respected yourself enough to leave him. With your next relationship you also stood up for yourself. During this stressful time you completed school and found a satisfying position. And you realized the dilemma you're in and came to see me."

"Wow, Ms G., you're making feel better. When I think about it, I have done a lot … I'm not the most confused person in the world. I have done something right like standing up for myself. I did finish school and even found a job. And now … now I'm starting a new life … a life with my baby."

• • • • • • • ● • • • • • • • •

Ms. Hedstrum was true to her word. She faithfully kept her appointments with her family doctor who endorsed what I already noted; Ms. Hedstrum was happily expecting and glowed with health. She had a rosy fullness in her cheeks and a skip in her walk. She continued to visit the office during the months of pregnancy. Besides counseling, I offered referrals to agencies providing maternity clothing and layettes which included necessities such as infant attire, diapers, bottles, formula and if she so wanted, information regarding nursing her baby.

As Ms. Hedstrum neared the final weeks, our time lessened. The phone call finally came. The delivery went smoothly—she had given birth to a lovely baby girl. She was settling into motherhood. After a maternity leave she planned to arrange childcare with family and return to work. I wished her well and offered future counseling services if she so desired.

My door is always open.

*Johnna Anne Gurr MS, LPC*

# ESSENTIAL MATTERS
## *Mountain Top View*

I love survival stories. What engrosses most is the how factor. How was the insurmountable conquered? A full cascade of inquiry ensues; the purposeful reasons of why, where the situation happened and when in history it took place. Attempting to answer these questions, I burn rapidly through the pages leaving scorch marks. I favor true survival accountings especially mountain climbing. I can't help it—if one appears on the library shelf, it finds it way on my lap. Personally I have only negotiated well-worn trails up little hills which is why these escapades are awesome. Unimaginable risk is embraced vicariously through these courageous mountaineers. I will probably not climb Mt. Everest, but that richness of experience gleaned by others is mine. All mine.

These stories begin with a kernel of expectation, a yearning to accomplish some task. They start with a simple thought like … "I will climb that mountain." From that hope filled thought the planning begins.

Dates are researched, fellow travelers are gathered. Costs are estimated and refined as crucial items such as camping gears and edibles are purchased, catalogued and stored. Training is assessed as levels of mountaineering expertise are expanded and honed. Transportation to these sites whether by sail, wheels or air are established. As the time nears a blend of angst and anticipation grows. Will they be able to commandeer this mountain? Is this a realistic goal or utterly ridiculous? How did they get themselves into this outlandish scheme?

And then again, why not?

The travelers are now making base camp—that lodging at the bottom of the mountain where the bulk of their provisions are stored. They ready what is absolutely necessary for their climb; the essential gear employed on varying levels of the mountain. Most important, the weather forecast is thoroughly considered for several days so to estimate uphill progress.

Ready. Set. Go. The team of mountaineers is off. Everything appears perfect; the weather, good health, enough provisions, a general upbeat attitude. The first day goes along without incident. The second follows suite. The third, well, let's say the mountain becomes an obstacle course. A surprise snowstorm with blizzard conditions hammers around them. Visibility is poor and footing on rocky surfaces is dangerously slippery. As they journeyed higher the air has become thin and some of the hikers become ill. Two men on the team have fallen and one was injured. Decisions vibrate with urgency—decisions that will make or break the climb. Team morale is low, many are weary and disgruntled. The hard choices are made—some will return to base camp for medical attention, the others will attempt to summit if and only if the weather improves.

Providence smiles on the remaining travelers. The next day, they continue their way up. Climbing is extremely strenuous and muscles are screaming out in fatigue. They trudge onward, the peak is within sight! Almost there. Wishing they could run instead of walk made their final trek almost unbearable.

Almost.

They stood at the summit. Silence. They gazed in awe. Then jubilant as they laughed and congratulated one other. Moments—that would become a lifetime memory—passed as they turned to descend. They paused only to look up and anticipate the next adventure.

Yes, I too travel down that snowy path, wanting for more.

Character cannot be developed in ease and quiet. Only through experience in trial and suffering can the soul be strengthened, vision cleared, ambition inspired, and success achieved.

                                                          Helen Keller

# Chapter Twenty

## Petticoats And Sidewalks

The crinoline petticoat arched the soft folds of the blue shirt waist dress. She removed her button down cardigan and swiped the sweat off her neck. The tawny Autumn like morning had morphed into a hazy humid afternoon. Dragging the sweater with one hand she clenched her lunchbox with the other. Contained inside the plaid metal box were leftovers of a peanut butter and jelly sandwich she had carefully prepared that morning. Looking down at her brand new penny loafers, she walked faster and faster. Then she hesitated and looked around. Nothing was familiar. The houses and the street signs were all wrong. Her heart was fluttering like a scared bird. She felt a knot in her throat and an ache in her tummy. The sweat was now running down the bodice of her dress causing the starchy fibers to itch.

She was terribly lost.

All she wanted was to find her house. Instead she had ventured deeper into the clapboard jungle. She would never find that bright yellow duplex she called home. Suddenly she felt nauseous—she could taste an odd sweetness from her lunch. Hands felt slimy and her right toe was blistering in the new shoes. Her green eyes pinched and grew wet. She had hoped to look brave as she held back the tears.

She was five years old and this was her first day of kindergarten. The young girl found a peeling gray bench that faced the street and plopped herself down. She was so sad, so confused. Bending her head, her natural curls encircling her face, she allowed the tears to fall. How did she get so lost? How would she ever get home? After all, this morning she had found the school yard all by herself. On her own, she had also washed, dressed and packed lunch. She was a girl who could find her way. Her mom and dad had said that the school was down the street. It was easy, they said. She remembered there were lots of turns and she had felt light headed. Still she had found the school. And she had been quite proud.

Her world had just collapsed.

A voice was calling. It was a kind voice and coming from behind her. She shifted her perch on the bench and saw a woman in the second floor window of an enormous white house.

"Little girl, is there something the matter? Can I help you? Just stay right there and I will come down."

The girl in the blue dress gasped. A *stranger* was talking to her! Her parents had told her *to never, never talk to one*. Icy pricks of terror ran up and down her spine. A blast of energy ejected her off the bench as she sprinted down the street. Her heart was pounding, pounding. Teeth were clanging in her mouth. She watched as her leather shoes carried her and somehow that big toe didn't hurt anymore.

She stopped. Looking up she saw Brickford Avenue, her street. With a shout of glee she rushed to the house and let herself in,

• • • • • • • ● • • • • • • •

I was this little girl.

This final account is about me. This is the last chapter of assorted stories that have been shared. I write about myself, not a composite personality, and relate an actual incident described as best remembered. I thought it would be interesting to share my story with you, dear reader who has finished this far in the text. Such disclosure may also happen within the counseling relationship. As you detail your situation, I may interject some of my own; but only if this disclosure will provide clarity and forward movement—which I hope happens now.

Realizing responsibility at a young age I managed—with a great deal of stumbling around—to find solutions. My parents never knew of my "almost" misadventure of walking home. I wasn't going to tell them. They were busy—Dad maintained his own car business and Mom spent hours in her room. If they thought I could do it, I didn't want to prove them wrong and look silly. Sometimes I felt like the tender leafed plant that had been stuck on the porch to harden off, to become strong. After a long while, I, like this plant, was anchored in the open garden subjected to the cold, downpours and gusty winds. With the right conditions including sunshine and gentle rain, the tiny seedling—me—produced the flower and fruit any farmer would applaud. Not just surviving but thriving.

Yes, that day is etched in my memory. There were decisions to be made and sometimes I was frightened and anxious, but personal tenacity and strength pushed me forward. I wanted to go to school and that was that. So off I went. Yet on the way to success obstacles can push one off course. Such it was with the first day of school—there I sat on that bench, scared and sobbing wondering which way to go.

Determination propelled me then and now. I was willing to plow through unwieldy territory to achieve desired goals. Headstrong, there was an attempt at singular effort. However I have come to realize others were plowing beside me, offering wise directives. Such mentoring came in many forms. Selected family members, friends and acquaintances offered support. Most appreciated were those teachers, co-workers and supervisors who provided direction and guidance.

Books became a constant companion; their authors my heroes. I absorbed stories of turmoil and angst as writers expertly turned woes into enticing wonderment. Shelf upon shelf of biographies as well as faith–based manuals and research materials line the walls in my home, their contents putting bounce in my shoe.

When overwhelming situations attempted to undo me, I chose to take a seat with a wise, empathetic counselor. Sifting through life's struggles with professional attentiveness was welcomed. Counseling made the difference.

In part, I realize the person I have become happened on that bench. Life decisions faced me—to decide to move forward or back; to take a moment and think things out. And to understand that others can help, even if that supportive hand gives us a swift kick off the bench.

But I found home.

Only a thumbnail of disclosure has been shared with you. Purposely so. A plethora of savory events have not been detailed. There is yet much to be said—of earlier years filled with a dysfunctional family, of teenage crisis seen in an abrupt departure from home, of college survival living month after month on stone soup. Yes, only a plain ham and cheese sandwich has been offered. No condiment, pickles, lettuce or tomato. Or bag of chips and fancy chocolate cupcake.

Stated are the basic essentials. Why, you ask?

Because well, that would make for good reading in another story, don't you think?

www.ingramcontent.com/pod-product-compliance
Lightning Source LLC
Chambersburg PA
CBHW030001091225
36532CB00038B/404